Queer Wars

Queer Wars

The New Global Polarization
over Gay Rights

DENNIS ALTMAN AND
JONATHAN SYMONS

polity

Copyright © Dennis Altman and Jonathan Symons 2016

The right of Dennis Altman and Jonathan Symons to be identified as Author of this Work has been asserted in accordance with the UK Copyright, Designs and Patents Act 1988.

First published in 2016 by Polity Press

Polity Press
65 Bridge Street
Cambridge CB2 1UR, UK

Polity Press
350 Main Street
Malden, MA 02148, USA

All rights reserved. Except for the quotation of short passages for the purpose of criticism and review, no part of this publication may be reproduced, stored in a retrieval system, or transmitted, in any form or by any means, electronic, mechanical, photocopying, recording or otherwise, without the prior permission of the publisher.

ISBN: 9780745698687
ISBN: 9780745698694

Library of Congress Cataloging-in-Publication Data

Names: Altman, Dennis, 1943– author. | Symons, Jonathan, 1976– author.
Title: Queer wars : the new global polarization over gay rights /
    Dennis Altman, Jonathan Symons.
Description: Cambridge, UK ; Malden, MA : Polity Press, 2016. | Includes
    bibliographical references and index.
Identifiers: LCCN 2015030522| ISBN 9780745698687 (hardback : alk.
    paper) | ISBN 9780745698694 (pbk. : alk. paper)
Subjects: LCSH: Gay rights. | Gays–Political activity. | Human rights.
Classification: LCC HQ76.5 .A39 2016 | DDC 323.3/264–dc23 LC record
available at http://lccn.loc.gov/2015030522

A catalogue record for this book is available from the British Library.

Typeset in 11 on 15 pt AGaramond
by Toppan Best-set Premedia Limited
Printed and bound in the United Kingdom by Clays Ltd, St Ives plc

The publisher has used its best endeavours to ensure that the URLs for external websites referred to in this book are correct and active at the time of going to press. However, the publisher has no responsibility for the websites and can make no guarantee that a site will remain live or that the content is or will remain appropriate.

Every effort has been made to trace all copyright holders, but if any have been inadvertently overlooked the publisher will be pleased to include any necessary credits in any subsequent reprint or edition.

For further information on Polity, visit our website: politybooks.com

CONTENTS

ACKNOWLEDGEMENTS

The authors are grateful to participants in two workshops, one at La Trobe University in 2013 and one in Los Angeles in 2014, where some of these ideas were thrashed out. There are too many participants to name them all, but special thanks to Sofia Gruskin, with fond memories of the walk in Washington Heights with Dennis that led to the Los Angeles workshop. Some of the ideas outlined here were first published in an article titled 'International norm polarization: sexuality as a subject of human rights protection'. published in the journal *International Theory* in 2015. We thank the journal editors and anonymous referees for their contributions.

Many other individuals and organizations deserve thanks, and their work is often reflected in our notes. Colleagues and activists across the world have been generous with feedback and information: thanks to Peter Aggleton, Paul Amar, Chris Beyrer, Tom Boellstorff, Christophe Broqua, Edwin Cameron, Carolyn D'Cruz, Laurie Essig, Gillian Fletcher, Masha Gessen,

Kate Gleeson, Aeyal Gross, Michael Kirby, Anthony Langlois, Terry Macdonald, Rafael Perez Munoz, Dede Oetomo, Jeff O'Malley, Richard Parker, Momin Rahman, Rahul Rao, Chris Roche, Hakan Seckinelgin, Jessica Stern, Maurice Tomlinson, John Treat, George Vasilev and Dennis Wang Yip.

We have gained valuable insights from groups such as the International Gay and Lesbian Human Rights Commission, the Global Forum on MSM and HIV, and organizers at the International AIDS Conference in Washington (2012) and Melbourne (2014).

Our editors at Polity, Andrea Drugan and then Elen Griffiths, have been both generous and encouraging, and we received helpful comments from two anonymous readers.

Queer wars: how should we respond to global polarization over gay rights?

When Conchita Wurst won the 2014 Eurovision Song Contest, Russian deputy prime minister Dmitry Rogozin tweeted that Eurovision 'showed supporters of European integration their European future – a bearded girl'. The contest took place against a political backdrop of rising tension between Russia and the European Union, Russia's passing of anti-gay-propaganda laws, the annexation of Crimea and continuing fighting in Ukraine by pro-Russian rebels. In Copenhagen the crowd booed Russia's entry, the Tolmachevy Sisters (winners of the junior Eurovision who had identified themselves as virgins in press interviews), while Russian audiences jeered the victory of a 25-year-old, bearded, Austrian drag queen. There were petitions against Wurst in Russia, Belarus and Armenia, despite her polling well in their popular vote. Wurst herself explained, 'I really felt like tonight, Europe showed that we are a unity full of respect and tolerance', and when asked for a message for Putin, replied 'we are unstoppable'. She emerged from this divisive contest as an instant symbol of sexual and gender diversity, much as had the Israeli transsexual, Dana International, who won the contest in 1998.

The divisions performed by the Eurovision crowds are more than symbolic. Every year thousands of people are beaten, harassed, raped and even killed because of their real or perceived sexual or gender 'deviations'. It is impossible to give accurate figures, as often the worst abuses are performed by the state, or at least ignored by authorities, as in the case of attacks on homosexuals by vigilante groups in Russia or the widespread 'corrective rape' of women perceived to be lesbian in South Africa.[1]

Sometimes abuses receive international attention, as in the case of David Kato, a prominent Ugandan gay activist who was murdered in 2011 shortly after winning a law suit against a local magazine which had identified him as gay and called for his execution. At his funeral activists grabbed the microphone to stop the Christian minister preaching against gays and lesbians. Over the next few years the Ugandan Parliament made various attempts to strengthen anti-homosexual legislation, which led to considerable US and European pressure on the Ugandan authorities. The film *Born This Way* (2013) shows the constant threats and persecution faced by homosexuals in Cameroon, a country which allegedly arrests more people for homosexuality than any other. A small group of activists have tried to build a movement there; some of them have now left, seeking asylum in countries where their lives will not be at risk. Like many women and men from Iran, Russia, Uganda and many other countries, they have discovered that to be open about one's sexual orientation, and even more often one's gender expression, is to face ongoing harassment, violence and even the possibility of being killed. Even in the most liberal of countries there is considerable violence and hatred directed at people who are seen as sexually and gender diverse.

We are writing this book in a time when one can point to huge gains in acceptance as well as major setbacks for the cause of gay rights, and sexual rights more generally. We seek to answer two questions: first, why, as homosexuality has become more visible globally, have reactions to sexual and gender diversity become so polarized? Both advocates for and opponents of sexual rights are passionate in their views, leading to a hardening of positions on both sides and the danger that arguments about sexual rights will be perceived as an inevitable cultural clash between western democracies and 'the rest', often countries struggling with colonial legacies or other forms of social disorder. Amid such polarization both sides lose sight of history; advocates tend to forget how recent are the advances in the west, while their opponents deny the long existence of various forms of sexual and gender diversity in their own cultures.

The book's second question is: what is to be done? As writers who believe passionately in the right of people to choose how they love and how they present themselves, we are equally concerned to think through how we can best achieve these rights globally. Over the past few years there has been a great deal of activity through international fora, as queer and human rights groups, increasingly with government support, have sought to address the situation of people often referred to as 'sexual minorities'. The decision in June 2015 of the US Supreme Court to grant constitutional protection for same-sex marriages (in *Obergefell v. Hodges*) has meant renewed international attention to questions of sexual rights. That same week authorities in Istanbul unexpectedly clamped down violently on a gay pride parade, a sharp contrast to the rainbow lights that illuminated the White House. In September 2015 the United States and Chile organized the first (informal) discussion of LGBT human rights in the UN Security Council in response to reports of Islamic State (ISIS) killings of homosexuals. Seemingly in response, ISIS immediately publicized several more executions of homosexuals.

Writing from the privileged safety of a liberal-democratic state, we are aware that advocates of international change must be cautious in urging action upon others. We might advocate radical arguments within our own communities that we are simply not entitled to make in the international context where other people live with the consequences. Our conclusion – that western advocacy should focus on building an international consensus protecting sexual minorities from violence and persecution – may seem minimalist, but it stems from respect for pluralism and a concern for the safety of people facing real threats of violence and intimidation. While we should offer support and solidarity for activists internationally on terms that they request, and while we can hope that basic protections will create conditions for more radical social change, we do not believe it is productive to try to impose human rights protections or that we can be radical for other people.

Finally, a brief note on the terminology used in this book, except when we are quoting others. 'Gay rights' (which are usually understood to include women as well as men) and 'LGBT rights' have become widely used, even though they link ideas of universal human rights with specifically western identities. 'LGBT' stands for 'lesbian, gay, bisexual and trans'; Australian usage adds 'intersex', but we are uneasy with the assumptions of specific identities underlying these terms. As Robert Lorway wrote of Namibia: 'Local gender and sexual knowledge becomes repositioned as *undifferentiated* – that is, not fully recognized and in need of elevation to the more secure status of LGBT identities.'[2] In contrast, most United Nations human rights documents refer to 'sexual orientation and gender identity' (SOGI) in order to recognize sexual diversity without prescribing specific identities, and at times we refer to 'SOGI rights' when discussing developments in international human rights practice. The term 'sexual minorities', which is sometimes used, assumes a common sense of identity and community that is only applicable to a relatively small number of people, while 'queer rights', which encompasses both homosexuality and gender expression, is more inclusive but overly academic. Further, while we recognize the problems of referring to 'the west', we use it as a convenient shorthand for grouping together the liberal democracies of Europe, North America and Australasia.

In reality, the goal of campaigns for 'queer rights' is the universal application of human rights, irrespective of sexual orientation or gender identity, and many have argued that this is better pursued through building protection for the 'sexual freedoms and rights' of all people. The very concept of 'sexual rights' was born from a feminist critique which rightly saw the subordination of women and the denial of the right to control their bodies as central to both social justice and genuine 'development'. Gay rights cannot be conceptualized without reference to broader concerns for sexual rights and gender equality (including a recognition of diverse forms of gender expression), but the major focus of the book is on the peculiarities of the contemporary international debates about homosexuality, and the ways these have come to stand for broader debates about culture, tradition and human rights.

ONE

Setting the agenda

It is tempting to see a new Cold War being played out around homosexuality. In 2014 the Winter Olympic Games took place at Sochi on the Russian Black Sea. The Games were carefully planned to enhance the reputation of Russia and its newly (re-)elected president, Vladimir Putin. But they followed the introduction of anti-homosexual-propaganda laws, disguised as protecting cultural values,[1] which in turn led to calls for boycotts of both the Games and some of the major corporate sponsors.

No country refused to participate in the Sochi Games, but the United States made its attitude clear by not sending any high-ranking official, and naming a delegation headed by several openly lesbian and gay sporting figures, including tennis player Billie Jean King. Other major political leaders and most European royalty also refused to attend the opening ceremony, although the king and queen of the Netherlands, flanked by Britain's Princess Anne and members of the Monaquesque and Luxembourgeois royal families, were present. The Dutch decision was somewhat surprising, given the extent to which the country has been a leader in promoting gay rights, and came in for some criticism at home. Nor were attempted boycotts always successful; a seemingly spontaneous boycott of Stolichnaya vodka collapsed when it became clear that the vodka actually came from Latvia, not Russia. Following the Sochi Games the International Olympic Committee announced new rules for the selection of host cities, including a requirement of full non-discrimination, which have yet to be tested.

In the controversies over Sochi and Eurovision one could see cultural battles around gay rights attaining a new international prominence. Such a coordinated international campaign around gay rights in an authoritarian country is unprecedented, even if the protests around Sochi were essentially symbolic. But homosexuality is constantly in the news. In one random day as we started writing this book (30 August 2014) the local Australian press carried stories about the first openly gay member of the Chilean navy, and commentary on same-sex marriage, alongside stories about the brutal lashings of a Saudi man caught using his Twitter account to arrange dates with other men. Not only do these stories point to the role of the state in regulating sexuality, they also underline the extent to which both public attitudes and state control appear to be moving in different directions in different parts of the world.

During the Cold War one of the few things on which both Soviets and the United States could agree was that homosexuality was a dangerous perversion. Indeed both countries saw an increasing fear and rejection around homosexuality in the 1950s, following a brief period after the Russian Revolution when the Soviets seemed to pursue greater tolerance, and the greater sexual freedoms that emerged in the United States after World War II. By the 1970s the social and cultural changes which are loosely associated with 'the sixties' had begun to challenge the dominant assumptions in most western countries that homosexuality was an illness, a sickness or a deviance. The Soviet Union was far slower to move in this direction, and although small gay movements emerged in a few non-western countries, homosexuality, indeed any deviation from 'traditional' assumptions about sexuality and gender, remained heavily stigmatized. While there have been huge shifts in general views of sexuality in the United States this century – epitomized in increasing support for same-sex marriage – the Putin regime has drawn on both the Stalinist and Orthodox traditions to increase persecution of people on the basis of their homosexuality.

After the re-election of both President Obama and President Putin (the latter after an obligatory period as prime minister) homosexuality emerged as a possible theme of a cultural Cold War. Both governments used queer rights as a weapon to mobilize international opinion, Obama using the language of human rights as against Putin's invocation of traditional *cultural* values. In the Russian rhetoric directed at Ukraine during the conflicts of 2014 there was a consistent strain of defending 'tradition' against the homosexual degeneracy of the European Union.

In October 2014, the *Economist* magazine, which is an extremely influential mouthpiece of liberal thought, published a cover story titled 'The Gay Divide'. The lead article described change in attitudes to homosexuality, particularly in the west, Latin America and China, as 'one of the wonders of the world'. Just why these changes have occurred so rapidly is a product of a number of factors, including the development of far greater gender equity, affluence and new understandings of human rights. These changes have not occurred without some backlash, as in various legislative proposals in the United States in reaction to growing support for same-sex marriage that seek to allow businesses to refuse services to 'LGBT people' in the name of religious freedom.

Yet the *Economist* also pointed to a growing global divide, in which homosexual behaviour was illegal in seventy-eight countries and punishable by death in about eight. While countries in Europe and the Americas have moved towards including sexuality in anti-discrimination legislation and legalizing same-sex marriage, other parts of the world have seen a dramatic increase in state-sanctioned homophobia. Legislation aimed at further restricting homosexual activity, often under the guise of protecting traditional values and families, has been introduced in a number of countries, and there are reports of increased violence against both homosexuals and trans* people, including rape, murder and torture. (The term 'trans*' refers to the full diversity of transgender, non-binary and gender non-conforming identities.)

The *Economist* story concluded that '[f]or those who cling to the notion of progress, it is hard to believe that tolerance will not spread'. But progress is never inevitable, and there are many parts of the contemporary world where there appears to be a retreat from notions of individual freedoms and human rights in favour of extreme religiosity or state authoritarianism. Most authoritarian regimes target sexually and gender diverse people, or, at best, refuse to protect them against abuse, although this seems least apparent in the countries of east Asia. The increased salience of sexuality means that LGBT rights are increasingly targeted by authoritarian governments for symbolic purposes, as in the crackdown on Istanbul's pride march in 2015.

One might question the *Economist*'s claim that China's acceptance of homosexuality is a 'wonder of the world', although there have undoubtedly been major shifts since the sexually repressive period of the Cultural Revolution, when homosexuality was officially regarded as a mental illness and a species of 'hooliganism'. Certainly the growth of affluence and urbanization has made it possible for some men, and fewer women, to live more openly as homosexual, and a new identity emerged, sometimes called *tongzhi*, a term which links traditional concepts of sexual and gender non-conformity to a global queer identity.[2] The Chinese Psychiatric Association removed homosexuality from its list of mental illnesses in 2001, and there is a visible queer world in major cities. However, this is available to relatively small numbers of Chinese, and many homosexuals enter into heterosexual marriages – sometimes between a lesbian and a gay man – to satisfy the dominant pressure from family and society. Nor are Chinese authorities sympathetic to anything which might look like a gay political movement, although there is official tolerance of social networks.

Other than Russia, no country has attracted so much attention for its anti-homosexual policies as Uganda. Like other former British colonies Uganda retained the colonial-era laws against 'carnal knowledge against the order of nature'; in 2005 it adopted a Constitutional amendment prohibiting 'marriage between persons of the same sex', even though no one in Uganda was advocating such marriages. Under pressure from both local and American Protestant evangelists Uganda moved away from successful condom promotions as part of the earlier response to HIV to a policy of abstinence before marriage, and anti-homosexual rhetoric grew dramatically. In 2009 an 'anti-homosexual bill' was introduced into the Ugandan Parliament with draconian penalties; debate around this Bill drew international attention, and it was finally passed in 2013, after considerable anti-homosexual violence including the murder of gay activist David Kato. After that law was annulled by the High Court on technical grounds, new legislation was introduced despite strong international condemnation.

One of the reasons the Ugandan case received such attention was that it led British prime minister David Cameron to speak of cutting development assistance to countries which did not respect gay rights, unleashing considerable protest from both governments and civil society groups in Africa and the Caribbean. Cameron's statement was particularly significant because it came in connection with a Commonwealth Heads of Government meeting (Perth 2011) where clear divisions emerged over decriminalization of homosexuality, a live issue in most countries of the Commonwealth. Along with statements by Secretary Clinton and President Obama it marks a new period in the international debate around sexual rights, even though Cameron failed to follow through on the threat in any organized way. 'Aid conditionality' has a long history (which we discuss later), but it is only recently that donor governments have sought to link development assistance to support for gay rights.

Why homosexuality?

There are specific reasons that help account for the unprecedented international attention to homosexuality in this century, but they grow out of a very long and complex history of preoccupation with all forms of unconventional sexuality. What today is referred to as 'queer', which we understand to mean the questioning of taken-for-granted assumptions about 'natural' gender expression and sexual identities, threatens conventional authority and beliefs. Sexuality is both separate from and inextricably entwined with gender: and it is only under certain conditions that homosexuality has not been confused with a rejection of traditional gender roles. (The most striking example is the honouring of male–male relations in certain warrior traditions, or the use of homosexual relations in rituals of masculinity.)[3] We are drawn to Diane Richardson's metaphor of seeing sexuality and gender as 'a shoreline...a boundary that far from being self-contained is extensive and shaped by the hinterlands that shape and shift it'.[4]

With a few exceptions, human societies adopt various forms of distinction between 'men' and 'women', which in turn are linked to their roles in reproduction. Within these limits all sorts of variations exist, and homosexual behaviour and desire are equally a feature of almost every society. What varies is how these are expressed, and how they are understood in relation to dominant assumptions about gender. Many societies have allowed for men – and less often women – to take on what would be understood today as a transgender role, dressing and behaving in ways that seemed to contradict their biological sex. Various forms of transgender identities existed across much of the world, including *hijra* in south Asia, *ashtime* in Ethiopia, *fa'fanine* in Polynesia or *berdache* among Native Americans. Often such persons are conceived of as belonging to a 'third sex', a concept that was taken up in the nineteenth century by such pioneers of sexology as Karl Ulrichs. The ways in which people perform gender roles – and the connections between these and sexual desire and behaviour – are complex and change over time, in ways that often defy easy generalizations.[5] In many cultures the basic divide has not been, as we assume, that between hetero and homo, but rather, at least for men, between 'active' and 'passive'; both Mediterranean and Latin American societies accepted that a man who took an 'active' role in intercourse was not therefore a 'real' homosexual. This is an attitude that persists among many young men who sell themselves to 'real' homosexuals while maintaining a sense that they are not, themselves, gay, sometimes by refusing certain forms of sexual activity.[6]

It is remarkable how many variations of the complex relations between sexuality and gender exist across time and space, and, equally, how all societies seek to regulate and limit these relations to support a dominant sense of what is 'natural'. The growing use of the term 'LGBTI' not only lumps together sexuality and gender, it imposes certain western assumptions about sex and gender as the basis of particular identities which may not leave space for other cultural traditions. While the term is embraced enthusiastically by some activists in non-western societies, others question it, as in Neil Garcia's claim that even as Filipino queer groups use the categories of western language 'residual indigenous valuations of gender have served to modify – that is to say, hybridize – the newly "implanted" sexual order'.[7] In Nepal some activists have consistently used the language of a third sex to embrace both homosexual and trans* expression. The term 'men who have sex with men' (MSM) is frequently used in the AIDS world to indicate that sexual behaviour and identity are not necessarily the same. (Similarly the term 'down low' has been used to describe this phenomenon in the African American community.)

Contemporary assumptions about homosexuality no longer link it as always implying a rejection of dominant gender roles; indeed many 'lipstick lesbians' and 'butch' gay men perform these roles to the extreme. At the same time there is an assertion by some transgendered people that it is unhelpful to conflate gender identity with sexual preference: being transgender or intersex (that is, born with non-differentiated sexual characteristics) does not tell us about sexual desires. A trans* person may seek to change their gender expression because of a desire for either women or men, or both, and the logic of gender fluidity calls into question the whole notion of a clear division between homosexuality and heterosexuality. In his book *Real Man Adventures*, T Cooper makes clear, perhaps too often, that the reason for his gender transition is his identity as 'a straight guy'.[8]

In some countries, above all Iran, it is assumed that homosexuals are people of the wrong gender, and they are strongly 'encouraged' to seek gender transitions. In western countries one sees something of an echo of this perception, as some prominent 'butch' lesbians now transition to become men, or claim an ongoing gender fluidity.[9] In many societies homosexual behaviour has been permissible, if not often acknowledged, as long as it does not interfere with the basic needs to reproduce and continue a biological family. It is usually only in conditions where individuals do not depend on their biological families for basic survival that homosexuality can become the basis for a primary identity, and the move from seeing homosexuality as a vice to which anyone might succumb to seeing it as an essential, if not immutable, identity is a product of nineteenth-century thinking. (Sociologists speak of 'master status', namely a sense of identity, often shaping a person's entire life; it can be based upon race, class, gender, religion or sexuality.) The very term 'homosexual' was coined in the 1860s in Germany, and became the basis for a new sense of identity based upon sexual attraction.[10]

While there are arguments about the exact time and place in which people started to identify themselves in terms of their sexuality, such identities seem linked to the development of capitalist and consumer society, allowing individuals the possibility of lives outside the extended family. This is evident from the co-existence of both 'traditional' and 'modern' notions of homosexuality in many parts of the world, which allows for different ways of understanding both erotic and emotional preferences.[11]

Until very recently it seemed that to be homosexual meant confinement to a marginalized and secretive life, often living in fear of violence, blackmail or imprisonment. Today increasing numbers of same-sex couples are seeking to reproduce nuclear family structures through marriage and children. Whereas the international community is increasingly divided over the criminalization of homosexual acts, many western activists have become preoccupied with securing a right to same-sex marriage, and this has become a high-profile political issue in many places.

The regulation of sexuality is often the occasion for considerable political disputes, and almost all religious and cultural traditions impose strict rules around what is and is not appropriate behaviour. The rules differ enormously; what seems also true is that hypocrisy is a common element of most sexual regimes. The most consistent regulation of sexuality concerns the rights of women, and in the contemporary world any discussion of queer sexuality has to recognize how it is inextricably bound up with the very different ways in which societies regulate female and male sexuality.

There is a long history of cultural contestation around sexuality, and of using sexual panics for political mobilization. For most of western history sexual pleasure has been viewed as secondary to marriage and reproduction, and women were commonly married off by their families, often for economic reasons, while men were often allowed considerable sexual pleasure outside marriage. Arranged marriage is a practice which continues today in many parts of the world, and leads to political conflicts between some immigrant communities and their new countries of settlement. Equally prostitution, usually, if incorrectly, conceptualized as only involving women selling sex to men, has been regulated if in very different ways in most societies, and remains a touchstone for political debate. Claims of 'a white slave trade' at the end of the nineteenth century, involving forced trafficking of European women into Argentina, was often linked to anti-Semitic rhetoric, and led the American Congress to pass the Mann Act, which gave police wide powers against 'debauchery'. In the contemporary world concerns about sex trafficking have been behind new moves to criminalize sex work, and, in some cases, those who seek to purchase sexual services.

Political homophobia

In the western world strictures against homosexuality have long been severe – Dante consigned sodomites to the seventh circle of Hell, along with blasphemers and usurers. Especially where Christian missionaries played a major role, European colonial powers saw homosexuality as a vice to be controlled, as part of the imposition of a civilizing influence. In the thirteenth century 'canonist' analysis of the legality of papal interference in infidel societies identified sexual violation of the natural law (sodomy) and mistreatment of Christian missionaries as the two circumstances that could justify military intervention.[12]

As European empires spread they brought a sexual morality based on an idealized notion of monogamous heterosexual marriage, which often clashed with deeply entrenched cultural practices. As part of the internalized sense of inferiority that colonialism created amongst many of those it governed, such restrictions often became redefined as part of national culture, with the odd result that today most of Britain's former colonies retain heavy sanctions against homosexual behaviour, even though Britain itself has long abolished these – and now urges its former colonies to do so. French colonies benefitted from the abolition of sodomy law through the Napoleonic Code, though some have subsequently adopted anti-homosexual laws since independence.

The need for cheap, often forced labour meant the creation of effective gender segregation, which worked against the creation of the stable nuclear families advocated in colonial rhetoric. All-male settlements of mine workers developed, for example, particularly in southern Africa, and inevitably so too did homosexual relations, and a practice of informal marriage between older and younger men.[13] During the nineteenth century the British held a strong belief that homosexuality was a particular vice of the tropics; Richard Burton, the British explorer and translator of the *Arabian Nights*, coined the term 'Sotadic zone', which rather oddly covered all of the Americas and excluded all but the northern fringes of Africa.

Increasingly homosexuality has come to stand in as a marker of deeper anxieties about aspects of western culture, economics and politics that threaten established authority, both religious and political, in many parts of the world. Homosexuality becomes linked with visions of women overthrowing traditional restraints, with widespread pornography and prostitution, but also with other fears of 'modernization' and 'westernization' destroying traditional families and religious beliefs. There are many examples of this, from the persecution of opposition leader Anwar Ibrahim for alleged sodomy in Malaysia (on two separate occasions over a sixteen-year period, involving several jail sentences) to the rhetoric of many African and Islamic leaders.

One of the few issues on which religious fundamentalists of all faiths can agree is opposition to homosexuality, and much contemporary anti-homosexual rhetoric is justified through particular interpretations of religious texts, even where it is driven by other factors. It is an oversimplification to posit attitudes to homosexuality as a significant divide between a rich liberal and a poorer authoritarian world, but it is true that there are few issues on which opinions seem as polarized, both between and within nations. In many western countries acceptance of homosexuality as other than a crime, an illness or a sin is recent; it was only in 2003 that the US Supreme Court overturned existing anti-sodomy laws in the United States, and many US states still do not provide for protection for people discriminated against on the basis of their sexuality or gender identity. The decision of the Supreme Court twelve years later to guarantee a right to same-sex marriage became a major rallying point for opponents of sexual equality, including most of the Republican candidates for the US presidency in 2016.

Some international relations scholars have explained previous changes in international attitudes and values by depicting the 'life-cycle' of international norms as a product of social dynamics within international politics. Just as teenagers dress to mark out their social status (as jocks, nerds etc.), so countries use norms to establish hierarchies and to signal group membership (as liberal democracies, Slavic etc.). Governments' desire to maintain their esteem and legitimacy in international society means that their norms will tend to shift in patterns that resemble fashions sweeping through a schoolyard. A trend such as women's voting was at first adopted by only a few countries in the late nineteenth century, but once a group of influential countries accepted female enfranchisement a 'tipping point' was reached, after which the norm cascaded through international society with increasingly less resistance. Today, there are only a very few nations (such as Saudi Arabia) that have not accepted the norm of female enfranchisement.

Unfortunately, knowledge that some norms 'cascade' internationally doesn't guarantee that homosexual equality will be accepted around the world. It is equally possible that sexuality may be an issue that continues to divide the international community for many decades into the future. Indeed international polarization over whaling may be a closer analogy than female enfranchisement. When the International Whaling Commission imposed a 'moratorium' on commercial whaling in 1986 it seemed that a new norm of whale 'preservation' would cascade through the international community. However, the backlash against this US-sponsored norm has proved long-lasting. Japan and Norway, among others, have come to demand that scientific resource-management, not preservation, must govern whaling and have stacked the International Whaling Commission with allies to ensure that 'scientific whaling' can continue. For some Japanese, whaling has taken on a symbolic significance as an expression of Japanese national identity and resistance to western domination. In many parts of the world repression of homosexuals may be acquiring a similar symbolism as an expression of national identity and defiance.[14]

Recognizing how state regulation of sexuality is influenced by international trends might help explain emerging patterns in domestic politics. There appears to be a widespread international adoption of what Tom Boellstorff, writing of Indonesia in the early 2000s, defined as 'political homophobia': 'an emergent cultural logic linking emotion, sexuality and political violence... making enraged violence against *gay* men [his italics] intelligible and socially efficacious'. [15] The stress on *political* or collective homophobia is important, as the term itself was coined to describe an individual fear of homosexuality, which is not necessarily involved in all cases of persecution.[16] More recent additions of terms such as 'biphobia' and 'transphobia' further confuse the individual fears, often rooted in personal insecurities, with persecution by the state and other institutions.

More recently Boellstorff has pointed to an emerging language of 'moral terrorism' in Indonesia, directed at gay groups, which has created 'a new emotional climate of fear and mistrust'.[17] To this we might add other examples, such as the widespread murders of trans* women in Central America, 'corrective rape' of women perceived to be lesbian in parts of Africa, beatings and murder of perceived homosexuals by right-wing vigilantes in Russia and new pressures to enforce sharia laws against homosexual behaviour. In all these cases there is an emphasis on 'traditional' divisions between masculinity and femininity, and on the heterosexual family as the only acceptable way of organizing sexuality and gender.

Boellstorff was drawing on an already rich discussion of the links between nationalism and a particularly heterosexual definition of gender, in which male homosexuality, in particular, is proscribed. This was already evident in European fascism, which extolled masculine solidarity and cracked down ruthlessly on homosexuality as a threat to both the masculinist order and reproduction.[18] This understanding of nationalism as linked to a patriarchal gender order emerges over and over again; as Emilio Bejel wrote of Castro's Cuba: 'Cuban nationhood has been defined, in part, by its rejection of gayness and queerness.'[19] In this argument, which emerges in different forms to explain contemporary attitudes in places as dissimilar as Jamaica, Armenia and Kenya, nationalism is equated with a strong gender divide, where leaders exemplify 'real' men – occasionally 'real women' – and encourage verbal, sometimes physical, abuse of those who do not conform to gender and sexual stereotypes. As President Mugabe tightened his hold over Zimbabwe he scapegoated the small homosexual organizations as un-African and responsible for many of the economic troubles of the country, paving the way for increasing homophobic rhetoric from a number of African leaders. (Despite this, when Canaan Banana, Zimbabwe's first post-independence president, was charged with sodomy and indecent assault, Mugabe's staff covered up his crimes and refused to assist his victims.)

Over a century ago Freud pointed to the connection between repression of homosexuality, particularly male homosexuality, and the preservation of certain forms of authoritarian structures. Presciently he singled out the church and the army, both of which are institutions that require very considerable male bonding while denying homosexual attraction.[20] Combined with the way in which acceptance of homosexuality is linked in the popular imagination to an undermining of masculinity, it is perhaps not surprising that homosexuality becomes a touchstone for so much anxiety in a period of global social change.

Homosexuality, and attitudes towards sexual and gender diversity, have entered mainstream global political debate in unprecedented ways. We need to distinguish between countries that officially recognize sexual and gender diversity and those that proscribe or actively oppose it; there are of course many examples where the official legal prohibitions are largely ineffective and other places where legal protection does not override social prohibitions. In turn the view of governments, as distinct from underlying attitudes, generally seems closely connected with support for cultural diversity of a wider sort and acceptance of a free civil society and liberal-democratic processes.

Globalization and sexual politics

How does the debate around queer rights relate to new forms of globalization – particularly the explosion of social media and electronic communications – and above all the rising profile of demands for human rights? Certainly globalization has made the diffusion of certain models of sexuality far more possible, and has facilitated the organization of both pro- and anti-queer-rights movements. As one author commented, 'When asked to date the beginning of the gay movement in Soweto, some young black men answered that it commenced when a gay character appeared on *Dynasty* on local South African television.'[21] In a similar vein Alyssa Howe writes that: 'In Nicaragua Amnesty International pamphlets condemning the anti-sodomy law...circulate alongside (very popular) screenings of "The Birdcage" on satellite TV. This pastiche of images and ideals, renders, over time, a homosexual and lesbian "identity" that is as familiar in Nicaragua as it is in other "local" settings including the North.'[22]

Activism is no longer constrained by geographic limits, and the internet has become a very powerful way of exploring and shaping people's imagination of their own sexuality and gender identities. The web has created new sites for sexual encounters, but even more so for the global dissemination of a language that cultivates sexuality-based identities. Both pro- and anti-gay-rights groups make extensive use of social media, but more importantly social media makes new images and possibilities available to people who previously would have had no access to them.

At the same time increasing religiosity in some parts of the world has led to an upsurge in anti-homosexual prejudice. While the Catholic Church under Pope Francis has softened its condemnation of homosexuality, many Christian churches, particularly in Africa, promote harsh criminal penalties for homosexual acts, and the Russian government's stance reflects that of the Orthodox Church. Almost all Islamic preachers regard homosexuality as a sin, and fundamentalist Islamic regimes are particularly harsh in their responses. Public executions, stoning and defenestration have all been reported as ways people perceived as homosexual have been treated in ISIS-controlled areas of Syria and Iraq. In India opposition to repealing anti-homosexual laws is strongly expressed by Hindu leaders, who have considerable influence within the ruling BJP.

As long as religious and political leaders continue to condemn sexual and gender diversity, this will invite interpretation as tacit support for prejudice, violence and persecution. Depending on where in the world one stands there is huge progress towards greater acceptance, or increased intolerance. Of course from the viewpoint of those who believe in 'traditional values' the gains and losses will often seem the reverse. But while there may be room for reasoned argument about the acceptance of same-sex marriage, the adoption of children or the most appropriate forms of support for adolescents who want to transition their gender status, there is never a justification for the use of torture, rape and murder of people because of their real – or perceived – deviation from what is assumed to be the 'normal'.

Awareness of sexuality, and of homosexuality in particular, is also a product of a global focus on AIDS, which peaked in the early years of this century, when AIDS became the first disease to generate special meetings of the UN Security Council and General Assembly.[23] Without the high-level attention that AIDS generated, much of the subsequent focus on gay rights would have been far less likely.

That AIDS was first identified amongst gay men in the United States – and for a short time was termed Gay Related Immune Deficiency – has created a permanent and complex relationship between HIV and homosexuality in the popular imagination. Even though a majority of global cases are due to infection through either heterosexual sex or shared injecting, rates of infection are very high amongst homosexual men, and stigma and concealment make reaching them with information and prevention often very difficult. While some governments have clearly taken on board the need to work with homosexual communities for effective HIV programmes, others have refused to do so, despite ongoing international pressure. There is a dilemma for advocates; in highlighting the risks of homosexual transmission they may also feed the worst sorts of homophobia. When a bathhouse was raided in Cairo in late 2014, and a large number of men arrested on charges of 'perversion', media reports spoke of 'the dens for spreading AIDS in Egypt'. Somewhat surprisingly most of the men arrested were acquitted by the courts, though the public humiliation remains.

Old and new politics have come together in unsuspected ways, as when American cultural conservatives

started justifying wars in Afghanistan and Iraq in terms
of liberating women. It is easy to read religiosity into
the cultural wars around sexuality – after all, this is the
ultimate authority to which both the Vatican and Iran
appeal – but how then do we explain the fact that there
is more acceptance of homosexuality in the Catholic
Iberian countries than there is in practice in countries
in east Asia, where organized religions are less
entrenched? Why is sexuality the site of so much anxiety,
as both Weber and Freud pointed out over a century
ago? Is speaking out strongly for gay rights, as is now
the practice of the US and other governments, helpful
– or does it, in practice, help fuel, even create, more
political homophobia? What to western eyes might
seem a basic assertion of human rights can easily be
portrayed in much of the world as echoing a colonial
language of a paternalistic civilizing mission. We recognize the concerns of one study from Rwanda which
argued that: 'Talking about LGBT rights as human
rights has not proved productive, therefore, and is
avoided by local organisations wherever possible.'[24]

It is tempting to argue that sexual diversity will only
be acknowledged and recognized in liberal-democratic
nations. Authoritarians have often linked homosexuality to democracy; the ruler of Belarus, Alexander
Lukashenko, once declared that 'It's better to be a

dictator than gay',[25] and the emergence of virulent right-wing parties in Hungary and Greece has been paralleled by a more open and virulent homophobic rhetoric. Both religious and political opponents of liberal democracy seem obsessed with homosexuality, as shown in the alleged comment by a leader of the fundamentalist rebel group in Nigeria, Boko Haram, that 'Democracy is worse than homosexuality, worse than sleeping with your mother.'[26] The connection he makes here reflects the salience of homosexuality in the contemporary political world, but it is important to disentangle the political from the cultural pressures involved. An opposite example comes from Israel, where the government has claimed its acceptance of queer rights helps distinguish Israeli democracy from the lack of human rights in the surrounding Arab world. This claim has led to bitter arguments around what Israel's opponents call 'pinkwashing', namely an attempt to distract from the illegality of Israeli occupation of much of Palestine through claims to accept sexual diversity.[27]

While support for sexual diversity has generally been associated with the left side of politics, the arguments around 'pinkwashing' suggest this is no longer automatically so. In the case of the Front National in France, the far-right group with growing electoral clout, there appear to be major divisions between supporters of gay rights, close to party leader Marine le Pen, and more traditionalist supporters. Claims that Marine is surrounded by a 'gay lobby' have been used to attack her from further right, and some influential gay figures have associated themselves with the party.[28]

TWO

The emergence of a global movement

While there is a century at least of political organizing around homosexuality, and recognizably gay and lesbian worlds existed in major western cities from the nineteenth century on, contemporary assumptions about homosexuality as the basis of an identity and a community, with the potential to organize for equal rights, really only date back to the late 1960s, and are a product of the huge cultural and economic shifts across the western world in that period.

The first organization to take up homosexual rights was founded in Germany by Magnus Hirschfeld at the very end of the nineteenth century, and continued in various forms until the Nazis came to power and began to imprison and then kill homosexuals. Small gay and lesbian groups developed after World War II in both western Europe and the United States, but it was not until the end of the 1960s that acknowledgement of equality for people regardless of their sexuality became the basis for a larger continuing social movement. Gay liberation was born out of the large-scale social and cultural change of the late 1960s and early 1970s, which was expressed through student, anti-war and black movements and, most crucially, what became known as the second wave of feminism.

The gay and lesbian movements of this period were largely formed by people who had been already politicized by other radical protests, and saw themselves as part of a broader new politics, aimed at transforming western societies. This was true of the small radical gay groups connected with the student uprisings of 1968 in Paris and Italy, and, though less completely, of the groups that formed after the famous raid on the Stonewall Inn in New York in 1969, which led to three nights of protests in Greenwich Village, the apocryphal birthplace of the gay liberation movement. Small liberationist groups were part of the general rise of political radicalism in some Latin American countries at the turn of the decade, although they were forced underground by the wave of dictatorships that swept the continent during the 1970s.[1] Particularly in the United States the first wave of radical activists would be quickly joined, if not supplanted, by others who sought recognition through respectability, and began to establish a set of institutions which turned the gay and lesbian movement into a significant political and economic force.

One of the distinguishing features of the gay movement, unlike the other radical groups of the period, was that it created not only communities but also markets. The 1970s saw a flourishing across the rich world of both homosexual activism and an expanding commercial world. Bars, discos, bookshops, publishing houses, gay male resorts and women's (sometimes womyn's) festivals aimed at a gay market flourished, and by the end of the decade were linked to an expanding network of community activities that were beginning to attract the attention of mainstream businesses. By the 1980s political fundraising directed at candidates sympathetic to gay causes had become a feature of American politics, heavily centred on the Democratic Party.

While activists were small in number, gay pride marches, originally meant to commemorate the events at Stonewall, began to attract hundreds of thousands and spread beyond their origins in the United States. By the 2000s various forms of gay pride rallies had become among the largest regular events to bring people out onto the streets – with the largest estimated numbers exceeding a million in São Paulo and Madrid. Huge gatherings such as these are often criticized by activists for their declining commitment to radical politics, with more mainstream and business participation, yet they also serve to entrench the concept of sexual minorities as communities deserving recognition, and are often the means whereby individuals feel first able to make a public declaration of their sexuality or gender expression.

Over a few decades what had begun as a fringe movement of predominantly young angry leftists grew into a significant social movement, not only in the United States and other rich English-speaking countries, but to varying degrees in every country where political space existed for organizing around sexuality. Even where homosexuality remains illegal, such as Singapore, this century has seen a flourishing movement; in 2014, 25,000 people attended the Pink Dot parade in Hong Lim Park, the only site in the city where such gatherings are allowed. In other parts of the world – Russia (see *Alekseyev v. Russia*, European Court of Human Rights, 2010); Serbia; Kenya – smaller events have been attacked by violent protestors, often with the complicity of the police.

Making visible what already exists is a powerful form of political activism: in some ways it underlines the strategy of non-violent protest, whose tactics leaders such as Gandhi and Martin Luther King used to point to the discrepancy between the rhetoric and reality of colonial and racist supremacy. The early chants of the gay movement – 'Come Out wherever you are'; 'Out of the Closets and Into the Streets' – were assaults on what remains the dominant mode of managing homosexuality in many societies: the social equivalent of the awkward moment of 'don't ask, don't tell' in the US military. Not surprisingly the idea of 'coming out' became a central organizing principle for people with AIDS when they started demanding inclusion in policy making during the early years of the epidemic.

The initial mobilization of thousands of people was around both a general demand for recognition and one for specific policy outcomes. In the English-speaking world the primary demand was to decriminalize homosexuality and to end police harassment. Even though laws against (male) homosexual behaviour were rarely enforced, they provided fertile ground for harassment, entrapment and blackmail, vividly caught in the 1961 British film *Victim*, which was sufficiently controversial to be banned for a time in the United States. Between the appearance of the Wolfenden Report in Britain in 1957, triggered by a number of prosecutions of homosexuals, which recommended that private consenting behaviour between men should no longer be a crime, and the decision of the United States Supreme court in 2003 (*Lawrence v. Texas*), which ruled that anti-sodomy laws were unconstitutional, almost all western countries removed homosexuality from the statute books, and in many cases introduced anti-discrimination protection.

In many cases decriminalization of same-sex activities had taken place quietly, often in the absence of a gay movement and as part of a general impulse for 'modernization'. In the fifty years following World War II there was a significant global wave of reform, which seemed to suggest a major shift away from regarding homosexuality as criminal. According to one study: 'In 64 of 72 cases sodomy laws disappeared or retreated during the post-World War period, with reforms decriminalizing sodomy, reducing homosexual ages of consent, or lessening punishments. The common thrust of the changes was very strong.'[2] While this study does not include all countries it certainly suggests a strong move towards greater liberalization, particularly in Europe and Latin America, with a marked move to decriminalization in the countries that emerged after the collapse of the Soviet Union in 1991.

Global activism

By the end of the 1970s gay movements were sufficiently established for tentative steps towards the creation of a global movement, which began with the founding of the International Lesbian and Gay Association (now known as the International Lesbian, Gay, Bisexual, Trans and Intersex Association) at a meeting in Britain in 1978. The organization has gradually grown to include organizations from over 100 countries, and relies largely on funding from the Netherlands and Nordic countries. It has played an ongoing role in lobbying international organizations such as the World Health Organization and Amnesty, and continues to bring together activists, particularly from within Europe. Meanwhile lesbian activists used the growing networks of international women's gatherings, including major meetings such as that at Beijing in 1995, to challenge assumptions of universal heteronormativity.

Over the past several decades a number of international queer advocacy groups have emerged, often with overlapping names in their boards and advisory committees. In 1990 a group of Americans established the International Gay and Lesbian Human Rights Commission (IGLHRC, which became OutRight Action International in 2015), working with 'people who experience discrimination or abuse on the basis of their sexual orientation, gender identity or expression'. IGLHRC, and the Canada- and Geneva-based ARC International, have provided support for groups across the world, and joined other human rights groups in lobbying UN agencies on sexual rights. Yet another international group, based in Paris, organizes the International Day against Homophobia, Transphobia and Biphobia, which also focuses on global discrimination. Of these IGLHRC is the best funded, and Ryan Thoreson has written a fascinating and detailed ethnographic study which details the ongoing tensions when a US-based group seeks both to become genuinely global, and to balance advocacy with working on immediate crises for individuals whose lives may be at risk because of their sexuality.[3]

As gay politics has become more salient outside the west, international movements have captured the attention of a number of well-established western organizations. The City of West Hollywood, which was established through a coalition of gay and other radical activists, has actively sought to build links with groups in the developing world, and major western LGBT organizations are focusing more on the realities of the huge gaps in empowerment that exist across the world. But it is probably through the various global institutions focused on HIV/AIDS that the most effective organizational support has been possible, meaning that debate around homosexuality is often framed as a public health issue.

In many countries the AIDS epidemic opened up possibilities for organizing and resourcing queer activism, which could be safely distanced by organizing around HIV information and prevention.[4] The Malaysian group, Pink Triangle, was established as an AIDS organization, despite the clear queer reference in its name. The M Coalition, based in Beirut, works across the Arab world and seeks 'an Arab world where the right to health and all other human rights of Men who have Sex with Men are recognized, realized and protected'. In the greater Mekong area, which includes several Chinese provinces, HIV has provided the possibility for cross-border organization through the Purple Sky Network, which has engaged both gay and trans men. There is a strong network of transgender women in Latin America, supported by the International HIV/AIDS Alliance, a significant HIV-focused non-governmental organization (NGO), which increasingly focuses on those groups most vulnerable to infection, including MSM and needle users.

While HIV opened up possibilities for queer space, linking the epidemic to gay assertion also risked greater demonization, and tended to make women even more invisible, as lesbian practices have rarely been implicated in the transmission of HIV. While lesbian groups were emerging in many parts of the world, they are easily overlooked, as international funders have been heavily focused on the public health aspects of working with vulnerable populations. AIDS activism has often seemed inseparable from gay activism, and has contributed to the development of an emerging group of professional and skilled international 'LGBT' activists, who have played crucial roles as brokers between local communities and international institutions.[5] Moreover, the priorities of HIV activists, often well connected to an international movement such as the Global Forum on MSM and HIV, have sometimes clashed with the needs of those for whom immediate survival is the major priority. This is a not uncommon problem when well-intentioned activists seek to apply models developed elsewhere. Writing of Namibia, Robert Lorway argues that the foreign-supported Rainbow Project 'not only inhibited important political possibilities, but sometimes also reinforced social inequalities'.[6] The emphasis of the project on law reform and legal changes often seemed irrelevant to young and poor Namibians struggling to survive, while fascinated by a particular identity politics that threatened to alienate them from family and community.

The history of gay/lesbian movements will always be intertwined with broader political and social issues, and must therefore be considered within national, and sometimes local, contexts. Even where broad generalizations seem possible – Scandinavian countries; the

Arab world; sub-Saharan Africa – there are significant national differences that will affect both the social and legal status of what are often referred to as sexual minorities. We have chosen to write briefly of developments in six countries (Australia, Spain, Cuba, India, South Africa and South Korea) to illustrate some of these specificities; but a different set of examples would produce a very different narrative of the intersection of ideas, movements and authority. These are not exhaustive accounts, but rather focus on the interplay of politics, culture and activism to trace different itineraries towards acceptance of diverse sexualities.

Queer movements will develop where there is both need and space; that is, where people feel sufficiently discriminated against to make their sexuality politically salient, but also where there is sufficient political and social space within which to organize. As one activist remarked of South Korea: 'Oppression is real and ubiquitous, yet invisible enough to make calls for advocating homosexuals' rights look "excessive" or "privileging".'[7]

Australia

In a number of western countries where homosexual activity (usually confined to men) was defined as criminal, social attitudes changed ahead of legal reform. Australia adopted Britain's laws prohibiting 'carnal intercourse against the order of nature', and shared the strong taboos on homosexuality that were typical of both Britain and the US until the end of the 1960s. Criminal legislation was a matter for individual states and territories, although the first serious challenges to the laws came in a debate in the federal Parliament.

Australia was frequently described as deeply heterosexist, a society in which the closeness of men (often referred to as 'mateship') disguised deep sexual repression and segregation between women and men. Like the rest of the English-speaking world it experienced a homosexual panic during the 1950s, and it lagged behind Britain and Canada in repealing criminal laws.[8] Nonetheless it also saw a quick emergence of gay and lesbian movements from the beginning of the 1970s, and increasing public support for homosexual law reform. Support for decriminalization rose from 22 per cent in 1967 to 68 per cent in 1976, a reflection of a general liberalization of attitudes in Australian society.[9]

Compared with the United States, which also lagged behind other nations in law reform, Australia has a weaker degree of religiosity, but a political culture that

lacks the rhetoric of rights and the Constitutional protection for them. While the final end of anti-sodomy
laws in the United States was achieved through judicial
means, in Australia, as in the United Kingdom, it
required parliamentary action – but in this case, in eight
separate jurisdictions. In the first two, namely South
Australia (1975) and the Australian Capital Territory
(1975), the initiative for change came essentially from
socially liberal politicians; in Victoria from a combination of changing attitudes and a progressive state leader
(1980); in Queensland (1990) and Western Australia
(1989) from governments which reluctantly accepted
federal pressure. Only in the largest state, New South
Wales (1984), was there a powerful and vocal movement which forced change; for several years that state
prohibited discrimination based on sexuality while
retaining its anti-sodomy laws. Most interesting is the
case of the smallest state, Tasmania, where law reform
was blocked for many years by an unrepresentative
upper house, leading to the emergence of a small but
very visible activist movement. As we discuss in the
following chapter, Tasmanian laws became the basis for
the first successful attempt to use the UN Human
Rights Committee to overturn anti-sodomy laws; ultimately the ruling was implemented by Commonwealth
(federal) legislation in 1994, which read:

Sexual conduct involving only consenting adults acting in private is not to be subject, by or under any law of the Commonwealth, a State or a Territory, to any arbitrary interference with privacy within the meaning of Article 17 of the International Covenant on Civil and Political Rights.

What is striking about the Australian case is that law reform both foreshadowed and followed changes in public attitudes; the first jurisdictions to act were probably ahead of public opinion, but by the 1980s the shifts were such that the remaining states were clearly catching up. By the beginning of the 1980s a visible gay and lesbian culture was established in all the major cities, with tentative support from mainstream media and more enthusiastic responses from some inner-city politicians and business. The growth of Sydney Gay and Lesbian Mardi Gras, which has become the largest night-time street event in the country, is symbolic of both the rapid growth of people prepared to celebrate a sexual identity and the changes in Australian society. Mardi Gras is now acknowledged as an integral part of Sydney life, and welcomed by government and business for the visitors and money it attracts to the city.

AIDS was a tragedy in Australia, as everywhere else, but it came when there was already an organized gay

Acceptance and Multiculturalism

The rapid shifts in Australian attitudes were in part a reflection of growing support for multiculturalism, a term introduced into Australian political rhetoric in the 1970s. While the term itself has been contested during periods of conservative government, the reality of a multi-racial and multi-ethnic society makes it easier for sexuality to be seen as just another variety of ethnic diversity, as is also true in Canada and the United States. This is not to deny the complexities of some immigrant societies, where some communities might well hold more hostile attitudes towards sexual diversity than those in the host country.

The best example of these tensions is found in the Netherlands, where opposition to immigration has sometimes been linked to fears that it will imperil Dutch acceptance of homosexuality. There is a certain irony in that tolerance in the Netherlands grew out of the need to establish mutual acceptance between Catholics, Protestants and humanists, leading to the 'pillarization' of Dutch society, which allowed for gay/lesbian communities to be seen as part of the larger social contract. Since the emergence of anti-Islamic and anti-immigrant politics, and in particular since the assassinations of right-wing politician Pim Fortuyn in 2002 and filmmaker Theo van Gogh two years later, concerns about the impact of migration upon Dutch acceptance of sexual diversity have led to very bitter political debates, as conservatives have seized upon gay rights as a marker of Dutch identity which is threat-ened by the prejudices within the Islamic population, to the consternation of some more radical queer activists.[10] There is a genuine dilemma here: homophobia is far stronger among sections of the Muslim population, but equally opposition to these views too easily turns into unreflective racism against anyone perceived as Muslim.

The reality that most Islamic societies appear to be very intolerant of homosexuality, despite their own rich his-tories of same-sex desire, creates particular problems for those Muslims who are seeking to change attitudes and win acceptance for gay identities. The sociologist Momin Rahman has pointed out: 'We have to approach the for-mation of Muslim homophobia *within* the context of Islamophobia rather than reduce it to a preexisting com-ponent of a pre-modern, monolithic Islamic culture.'[11] The assumption that all Islamists are necessarily anti-gay can become a self-reinforcing concept, especially when it is seized upon by right-wing politicians who prefer defend-ing 'LGBT people' to understanding the worldviews of practising Muslims.

community, and a federal government that proved remarkably accessible. Indeed for a time the Australian response, which also involved organizations 'repre-senting' sex workers and drug users, was seen as a progressive model to be followed by others. Importantly, the willingness of governments to fund organizations which grew out of gay communities, and worked directly with them, helped create a new class of professional workers whose sexuality was directly relevant to their professional lives.

Spain

In a few decades Spain has gone from being a deeply repressive society to one with a large and open queer world, far more so than any other country in Mediterranean Europe. During Franco's regime homosexuals (mostly males) were sent to special prisons called *galerías de invertidos* ('galleries of deviants'), but soon after the restoration of democracy in the late 1970s the anti-homosexual laws were abolished, and the existing small commercial world grew very quickly.[12] At the same time the cultural transformation, spearheaded by a group of artists known as La Movida, created an environment in which all sorts of radical ideas flourished. The general opening up of Spanish society, and the rapid changes in attitudes towards sexuality, were reflected in the films of Pedro Almodovar, which presented a world of drug, transgender and sexual experimentation following the collapse of dictatorship and Spain's rapid integration into Europe.

Beginning in Barcelona at the beginning of the 1970s, small radical gay groups sought to build links with anti-Franco, and in some cases separatist, movements. It is difficult to assess how far these groups, and the various protests that they organized from the late 1970s on, were central to the rapid changes in attitudes towards homosexuality, which were part of a much larger and fundamental shift in Spanish political culture. At the same time the rapid growth of a commercial gay world, linked to tourism in places such as Sitges and Benidorm, as well as the major cities, meant gay culture became increasingly visible in Spain. By the beginning of this century Madrid was the site for the largest gay pride parade in Europe, and Spain legalized same-sex marriage in 2005, the third country to do so. While the issue was contentious, there seems to be majority support, even though a majority of Spaniards identify as Catholic.

Although the influence of the Catholic Church remains potent – reflected in ongoing debates around abortion – it has not been successful in blocking major gains, including recognition not only of same-sex marriage but of same-sex adoption rights in the same year. As in some Latin American countries, one might suggest that the overthrow of a dictatorship closely linked to the Church opened up space for a politicization of sexuality that failed to occur to the same extent in countries such as Italy. The comparison with Poland is interesting; there the overthrow of dictatorship was closely aligned with the Church, and probably strengthened conservative moralities.[13] Debate around issues of sexuality there has tended to lag behind that in other European countries, although in recent years the political party Ruch Palikota has made queer issues central to its platform and succeeded in getting openly gay and trans parliamentarians elected.[14]

The onset of AIDS changed the nature of the gay movement in Spain, although less so than elsewhere. Unlike in most western countries, homosexual transmission accounted for a minority of HIV cases in Spain, where shared needles were more significant, and there was resistance from some elements of the gay movement to acknowledging HIV as a priority. But as is true elsewhere a new generation of activists developed, often concentrated on particular issues or representing different sections of a diverse queer community. Despite the very different historical background, Spain today has a flourishing gay world, with a diverse movement that is not dissimilar to those of the English-speaking world.[15]

Cuba

Cuba stands out as a country that both is authoritarian and has seen major shifts in attitudes towards homosexuality after a period of considerable repression. One of the standard tropes in discussing sexuality in Latin America is to note the importance of strongly defined gender roles, and the emphasis on masculinity as defined by taking an 'active' role in penetration rather than by whom one penetrates.[16] The situation in pre-Castro Cuba was rather similar to that across the continent: a small homosexual world, catering in part to tourists in search of sex, and considerable police and social repression. But the Communist revolution, unlike the democratic revolutions in other parts of Latin American twenty years later, only increased persecution, and some homosexuals were interned in forced labour camps along with others perceived as 'anti-social'. (The Cuban novelist Reinaldo Aenas, who fled Cuba and died in New York in 1990, wrote of this period in his novel *Before Night Falls*.) By the 1980s there was a noticeable softening in government attitudes, and the cautious emergence of a more visible Cuban gay world, although almost entirely limited to men.[17]

Almost uniquely, Cuba responded to AIDS through a policy of quarantine during the early stages of the epidemic, which may have contributed to low rates of infection. Even though the authorities were careful to stress that they feared a generalized epidemic, based upon the deployment of Cuban troops in Angola, there was inevitably stigma that linked the epidemic to the previous policies towards homosexuals, which some apologists for the Cuban system seem inclined to over-look.[18] Real change in attitudes towards homosexuality only came in this century, and is often attributed to the persistence of Castro's niece, Mariela, who has used her position as head of the National Centre for Sex Educa-tion to push for greater acceptance. This is an almost unique case of a powerful non-queer advocate, with intimate ties to the summit of power, and has occa-sioned considerable criticism from observers who claim she is effectively using her position to co-opt a potential source of opposition to the regime.[19] The case of Cuba also suggests that major shifts in policies can occur without a significant political movement, although whether this has achieved real changes in underlying attitudes remains more problematic.

It is instructive to compare the Cuban case with Nicaragua, where after the collapse of the leftist Sandinista government the right-wing government of

Violeta Chamorro introduced a repressive law targeting anyone 'who induces, promotes, propagandizes or
practices in scandalous form sexual intercourse between
persons of the same sex'. Three years later, after her
government was defeated, the law was repealed, due in
large part to a campaign by Nicaraguan activists.
Cymene Howe argues that the ongoing struggle for
sexual rights in Nicaragua can only be understood
through the complex political history of the previous
decades: 'Just as the Sandinista Revolution was a mixture
of political, social, and religious principles, sexual rights
activists have developed a similar kind of bricolage,
creatively appropriating and engaging a hybrid set of
political approaches.'[20]

India and south Asia

As in much of south and southeast Asia, there is a long
tradition in India of conceiving of gender and sexuality
in rather different ways from that of the west, in part
linked to a non-monotheist religious tradition in which
gods can exhibit traits of both genders. It is often argued
that historically India has allowed for a greater variety
of sexual and gender expressions than most western
cultures, even if contemporary India seems clearly

more repressive. At the same time India has retained a particular category of transgendered identities, most notably through the *hijra* identity, namely men who act out a ritualized feminine role and have often been castrated. Since 2014 Indian law has recognized a 'third gender', but so far has retained British laws penalizing 'carnal intercourse against the order of nature' (Section 377), which has generally been understood to refer to male homosexual behaviour. While this law is largely ignored, its existence remains of huge symbolic importance, and has been the target of considerable political and legal activity for the past two decades.

The emergence of an Indian lesbian/gay movement has been placed in the late 1980s, with the founding of the lesbian group Sakhi in Delhi and the magazine *Bombay Dost*, which still exists.[21] Concern around HIV spurred further activity, and the Naz Foundation, which worked amongst MSM, attracted considerable attention when four outreach workers in Lucknow were arrested in 2001 and charged with promotion of obscenity. What is striking is how quickly other groups, magazines and some sort of queer consciousness then developed, so that most major Indian cities now host queer film festivals and a variety of groups based on sexuality and gender expression. The continued existence of the colonial laws criminalizing homosexuality became a focal point for political organizing, leading to a successful court challenge in 2009; four years later the Indian Supreme Court reversed the Delhi High Court's decision, which was followed by reports of a number of arrests for homosexual behaviour.[22] The reversal was a major blow to global shifts away from defining homosexuality as a crime, and at the time of writing it is impossible to know whether further changes, through either judicial or legislative means, are likely.

Shortly after the Supreme Court found Section 377 constitutional (as applied to private, consensual, adult sexual activity), the same Court recognized the existence of a 'third gender', and ordered the government to provide transgender people with quotas in jobs and education in line with other minorities, as well as key amenities. That ruling, which parallels developments in other parts of south Asia, highlights the simultaneous existence of indigenous and imported notions of sexuality. South Asia has a range of queer movements, embracing people whose identities are primarily around gender expression and those who are heavily influenced by western models of gay/lesbian activism. (Thus the Humsafar Trust in Mumbai, which is a major provider of HIV-related services, identifies itself as a community organization of 'self-identified Gay men, MSM, Transgenders, Hijras and LBT persons'.) The ongoing pressures to reconcile 'tradition' and 'modernity', both of which are themselves constructs, mean that there are ongoing and sometimes bitter disputes about terminology and, in particular, to what extent homosexuality is itself part of a rejection of binary gender roles.

While Nepal has decriminalized homosexual behaviour and has debated a number of progressive measures, due largely to the leadership of Sunil Pant and the Blue Diamond Society – Pant became the first openly gay parliamentarian in the region[23] – the changes in India are probably more profound, at least in that part of the country that is integrated into the global economy, and linked through social media and language to a broader international queer world. The growth of discussion of homosexuality in Indian media – the first 'gay kiss' in an Indian film came in 2010 in *Dunno Y... Na Jaane Kyun* – reflects the ongoing tensions around open acknowledgement of sexuality in a society which is simultaneously erotic and puritanical, and in which a strong Hindu nationalism rejects contemporary expressions of homosexuality as alien to Indian culture.

The sexual conservatism in Bangladesh and Pakistan is clearly linked to Islam, but there are similar attitudes in Sri Lanka, which is a predominantly Buddhist society, and one with very strong social conservative values. In all three countries one can find small gay and lesbian groups, often supported by HIV programmes and external funders, but the reality for the great majority was summed up by a western activist after visiting Bangladesh:

> Homosexuality is not shunned because of its criminal tag; it simply does not exist in the common mind as a variant of human behaviour. This is a highly social culture with large and extended families, friends coming and going, eating and sleeping together at different times – all encased in strong social traditions. So what is this strange thing called gay love? Few have an answer.[24]

Across south Asia, above all in major centres such as Mumbai and Delhi, one finds increasingly visible groups of people who identify with global concepts of 'LGBT' identity, and are often well connected through travel and social media. The gap between them and the vast majority living in urban slums or rural areas who might experience same-sex desires and behaviour is huge, and will not be quickly bridged.

South Africa

Because laws are easier to quantify than social attitudes, many surveys of acceptance put South Africa, with its Constitutional guarantees around sexuality and recognized same-sex marriage, as amongst the most progressive countries in the world in its attitudes towards homosexuality. It is not that simple.

Under apartheid, homosexuality was deeply repressed and denied, even though it was well known to exist amongst segregated black mine workers and within certain closeted areas of the white population. In a society in which everything was racially defined, there were few commonalities between, say, a woman attracted to women in the affluent suburbs of northern Johannesburg and a young effeminate man in one of the huge townships that, as Mark Gevisser has so eloquently described, existed outside even the mental maps of white South Africans. As Gevisser writes: '"Queers" were as threatening to the white civilization as communists or miscegenating heterosexuals, and the state proposed legislation that would make it illegal to be homosexual.'[25] The deep fear and hatred of homosexuality in the apartheid regime are, ironically, one reason why South Africa appears to have followed a somewhat different path to the rest of sub-Saharan Africa.

Crucially, gay rights were incorporated into some of the rhetoric of the African National Congress before the end of apartheid, in large part because of the work of some gay individuals who were accepted as a legitimate part of the democratic struggle. Most important was Simon Nkoli, an openly gay political activist whose arrest and trial in 1984 attracted domestic and international attention. In the context of a new global language of rights the African National Congress adopted support of sexual rights in ways that would have been impossible for anti-colonial movements twenty years earlier. This does not deny a complex set of prejudices, both racial and sexual, which existed in South Africa, 'an amalgam of quasi-scientific postures, naturalised moral codes, historically rooted practices, displays of power, or distractions from political crises'.[26] There was a clear case of homophobic violence in actions connected with Mandela's second wife, Winnie Madikizela-Mandela, who was associated with alleged kidnapping and beatings in 1991.

Unlike the case in other post-colonial nations, where it has been easier to position 'sexual rights' as a legacy of colonialism, the dismantling of apartheid meant a need to accept diversity of ethnic and cultural communities, and was aided by a strong independent judiciary. In fact many of the legal advances have come through judicial rulings, which are not necessarily widely supported across the country. Thus the parliamentary vote to accept same-sex marriage followed a ruling by the Constitutional Court in 2005, even though there was almost certainly not popular support for the measure. Anti-gay violence, often expressed through rape of women perceived as lesbian – the term 'corrective rape' was coined in South Africa when a number of such cases took place in the early 2000s – is a reminder that law reform alone is insufficient, especially if it moves far ahead of social change. The high incidence of rape in South Africa, and strong homophobic rhetoric, appealing to both religious and nationalist masculinity, make the situation for women perceived as lesbian particularly dangerous.

The situation in South Africa is further complicated by the history of the AIDS epidemic. One of the country's great tragedies is that the end of apartheid coincided with the rapid increase of HIV, which, while first diagnosed amongst white gay men, very quickly reached epidemic scale through heterosexual transmission. While South Africa had by far the most developed health system on the continent, the politics of creating a new state also distorted the response to the epidemic in ways that were to prove tragic. President Mandela did not give AIDS the priority it required; his successor, Thabo Mbeki, became obsessed with finding 'African solutions', based on denying the reality of HIV and therefore of anti-retroviral treatments, almost certainly leading to tens of thousands of unnecessary deaths.

With his replacement by Jacob Zuma in 2009 there was a significant shift in policy, and therapies became far more widely available. Despite his denialism Mbeki showed no signs of wanting to scapegoat homosexuals for AIDS, and was supportive of the push for gay rights.

The anti-apartheid struggle meant that South Africa had a very active civil society, and lesbians and gay men have played a crucial role at certain key moments in ensuring inclusion in ongoing debates around the discourses of rights. While the queer world reflects the ongoing racial and class gulfs of contemporary South Africa, there is a significant commercial gay world, largely male, and particularly evident in Cape Town, which has made major efforts to market itself as a gay destination. The success of the gay movement in South Africa is closely bound up with its ability to reach beyond immediate issues of sexual minority rights and link them to broader concerns for social justice and survival. The Johannesburg-based Coalition of African Lesbians states that: 'We view ourselves as a part of social movements, including the women's movement, the sexual and reproductive rights movement, the broader lesbian, gay, bisexual, transgender and intersex movement and the economic justice movement.'[27]

South Africa's position in international debates is crucial, and there appears to be some conflict within government around the extent to which it is prepared to argue against most of its neighbours for protection of queer rights (neighbouring Mozambique's Parliament repealed colonial-era laws criminalizing homosexuality in December 2014). The country's queer movement needs to counteract strong 'Africanist' arguments within the governing structures, which would prefer to align South Africa with the dominant homophobic positions of most African governments.

South Korea and east Asia

The most commonly cited examples of repressive attitudes towards homosexuality are linked to authoritarian governments with a strong religious base; yes, there are democracies where governments remain repressive (e.g. all but the Bahamas among the independent, English-speaking countries in the Caribbean), but affluent liberal democracies are generally the most likely to accept sexual diversity. Of course we need be careful about making causal connections, as Richard Florida implies in his claim that 'The connection between attitudes towards gays and lesbians and economic development could not be clearer.'[28] That we should beware of too many such generalizations is clear when we look at the rich liberal democracies of east Asia. While there is clearly a gay world in cities such as Tokyo, Seoul, Singapore and Hong Kong, and a visible movement for recognition, especially in Taiwan and Singapore, attitudes towards homosexuality retain much of a Confucian framework in which expectations of conventional marriage and children are very strong. In Japan, which has seen a certain degree of activism – including a successful law suit against the Tokyo Metropolitan government, which had banned a young lesbian and gay group from using its premises (1991), and gay pride marches since the 1990s – the numbers mobilized by the movement remain small. The 2013 Gay Pride March in Tokyo was very small by international standards – even though it was joined by Akie Abe, wife of conservative prime minister Shinzo Abe – but in a sign of change Tokyo's Shibuya ward became the first place in the country to certify same-sex relationships in 2015.

In South Korea, which is rich, democratic and not particularly religious, homosexuality is culturally repressed, and the movement very small. Small lesbian and gay groups began to emerge in the mid-1990s, and in 1997 a Seoul Queer Film and Video Festival was initially banned by authorities; since then it has become an annual event. In 2008 an open lesbian ran, unsuccessfully, for the National Assembly, and since 2013 there has been an annual pride parade in Seoul, but despite being small it has attracted considerable opposition from evangelical Christians, who make up a sizeable minority. (Equally the Catholic Church, although its members comprise less than 10 per cent of the population, is both influential and very conservative.) While homosexual behaviour is not illegal except in the military, an important consideration given compulsory military service for all males, there is little open acknowledgement of sexual diversity, and being open is very difficult for most South Koreans.

South Korean society is marked by both a Confucian legacy and the reality of ongoing conflict with North Korea. All males complete two years of compulsory military service after high school, and are lethally proficient in taekwondo upon completion of their service. The virulent anti-Communism of the Cold War period lives on, with the South Korean political spectrum tilted heavily to the right. There is a discreet commercial gay world, but the great majority of queer South Koreans eschew any public declaration of identity. Research by the Pew Center shows growing acceptance of homosexuality, but it still remains far below that registered in all other countries of comparable wealth and liberal-democratic standing. However, the generational differences in attitudes are among the most marked in the world, which suggests major changes may well be occurring in South Korean attitudes. These changes are consistent with the sociological 'post-materialist values thesis', which suggests that each generation raised in conditions of material abundance is likely to be more supportive of equality and sexual rights. If accurate, this implies that South Korea's conservatism may partially reflect its relatively short experience of affluence.

Changes in attitudes towards and the regulation of homosexuality are the result of a complex interplay of various factors, which will vary according to the larger social, political and cultural environment. As Lynette Chua has pointed out for Singapore, there is a need for a certain 'pragmatic resistance' in developing advocacy, particularly within authoritarian states.[29] We have already noted that legal change, usually the abolition of laws criminalizing homosexuality, has often occurred without any significant pressure from local movements. But without some form of activism to stake a claim for both recognition and protection, and to put sexual diversity on the political agenda, there will be no genuine recognition of gay rights, even where, as in the case of Cuba, the changes are imposed from the top. Without a changing international environment the

Cuban government would not have acted as it has, even though this is unlikely to be acknowledged by the authorities.

The activism that began with a few solitary voices in the nineteenth century, and then exploded in the new radical movements from the 1970s on, was essential in the shift from understanding homosexuality as a deviance to be stigmatized to accepting it as a legitimate expression of human sexuality. That shift is of course uneven, and almost certainly not accepted by a global majority. Nevertheless, global activism has opened up possibilities for ways of imagining sexual and gender identities that were not possible before, and has created networks of support for those struggling to define themselves outside the conventional order.

Social movements seek to create a sense of communal belonging and identity while demanding action from external forces, and they will inevitably be divided along lines of gender, class and ideology. In the case of the queer movement this becomes clear in struggles over the full inclusion of women and trans* people, in debates over the relationship to broader social and political goals, and in attitudes towards AIDS, which remains the top priority for many gay men. The emphasis on same-sex marriage has divided those who seek integration into mainstream society from those who hold to a more radical conception of what queer politics might mean.

There appears to be no one explanation for changing attitudes towards homosexuality, but there are certain correlations that appear reasonably consistent. Societies that are accepting of sexual and gender diversity will also be those with greater equality between women and men; with a clear division between the religious and political spheres; with some version of a liberal-democratic political system; reasonably affluent; and likely to accept ethnic and racial pluralism. Note these are generalizations: none of them by themselves guarantee acceptance, and there will always be outliers. But reluctant as we are to suggest a linear narrative, there is a good argument for suggesting that a gay identity and community are both a product of and a marker of a certain sort of modernity.

THREE

Queer rights as human rights

US secretary of state Hillary Clinton's claim that 'gay rights are human rights', made at a landmark speech in 2011, reflects the view of most contemporary queer activists. However, many governments are so hostile that division over gay rights is undermining support for international human rights more generally. Opponents of 'sexual orientation and gender identity' rights claim that liberal western activists are creating a 'new category of persons' and that human rights are invalid if they conflict with the traditional values of mankind. These opponents note that the link between sexuality and human rights is relatively new. The Universal Declaration of Human Rights of 1948 ignored sexual freedom, and the language of human rights scarcely figured in the gay liberation movements of the 1970s. Nevertheless, developments in international human rights law, advocacy for women's rights, and political mobilization around HIV ultimately came together to make 'human rights' a central claim of queer politics.

The political theorist Charles Beitz identifies 'the central idea of international human rights' as the claim that 'a state's treatment of its own citizens is a matter of international concern'.[1] Whereas civil rights are claims against a specific political community, claims for human rights involve international society. To assert that 'gay rights are human rights' is to claim that persecution on the basis of 'sexual orientation and gender identity' warrants international concern. Given that homosexual acts are viewed as sinful by all major religious traditions, and are illegal in much of Africa, Asia and the Middle East, it is not surprising that such a sweeping claim by a US secretary of state was not universally welcomed.

Contemporary international human rights practice dates from the aftermath of World War II, when promoting 'human rights' was recognized in the United Nations Charter and then enumerated in the Universal Declaration. One factor prompting reluctant states to incorporate rights in the post-war settlement was revulsion towards Nazi crimes, particularly as articulated by American NGOs. Since homosexuals (wearing a pink triangle) numbered alongside Jews, Romani and Slavs as victims of the Holocaust, it might now seem strange that sexual orientation is not mentioned in the Universal Declaration or in either of the major Covenants on 'Civil and Political' or 'Economic, Social and Cultural' rights, adopted in 1966. However, Nazi targeting of homosexuals was not widely condemned or even acknowledged and the possibility of protecting sexual minorities was not considered.[2] Indeed some homosexuals were re-imprisoned by the occupying forces after the end of the war, and Nazi-era laws criminalizing all same-sex intimacy (paragraph 175 of the Criminal Code) remained in force in West Germany until 1969.[3]

While the negotiators of the major human rights agreements debated freedoms associated with heterosexual marriage and women's rights, no delegate even raised the possibility of protecting sexual orientation.[4] The concept of homosexuality was hardly unknown – certainly Eleanor Roosevelt, the first chairperson of the preliminary United Nations Commission on Human Rights (a body that was abolished and replaced by the UN Human Rights Council in 2006), was well aware of intimate same-sex relationships – but even she would presumably have regarded this as a matter of private behaviour not appropriate for discussion. As we have seen, the status of homosexuality as a social vice was one of the few issues on which the United States and the Soviet Union agreed in the late 1940s and 1950s, and similar attitudes were prevalent internationally.

Early radical campaigns for gay liberation mostly ignored human rights, although there were some echoes of human rights language in the earlier European homophile movements, such as Denmark's Kresden af 1948 ('The Circle of 1948').[5] Gay liberationists did not refer to 'human rights' but rather sought liberation by 'freeing ourselves' through consciousness raising, increasing visibility and building coalitions with other freedom movements. Legal tactics and rights claims later become more prominent when the radical gay liberation movement was eclipsed by groups, such as the US National Gay Task Force, that sought social acceptability rather than radical change. However, these reformist groups demanded *civil* rights from the nation-state, rather than recognition of universal 'human rights'. Human rights had not yet achieved a prominent place in public discourse.

Historian Samuel Moyn's claim that human rights were only invented in the mid-1970s, following the exhaustion of 'previously more appealing utopias', is probably a deliberate exaggeration.[6] Certainly, though, the political resonance of human rights has built incrementally over the past few decades and Moyn is correct to point to the mid-1970s – when human rights were embraced by eastern European dissidents and became a central plank of the Carter Administration's foreign policy – as an important turning point. The NGO 'Human Rights Watch' was first founded as 'Helsinki Watch' in 1978 (the Soviet Union guaranteed respect for human rights in the then Soviet bloc in the 1975 Helsinki Accords). Many influential academic programmes and human rights journals were also founded in the late 1970s and early 1980s. The growing prevalence of human rights discourse presumably explains why, in 1980, when the United States' first gay and lesbian 'political action committee' was established, it took the name 'The Human Rights Campaign Fund', although its actual mission was to promote civil rights and fund-raise for sympathetic political candidates.

Legal developments: sexuality and human rights law

Since early 'human rights' declarations and covenants made no reference to sexuality, they seemed irrelevant to the social transformations sought by the gay movement. However, once international legal mechanisms allowing individual complaints were established, these new human rights instruments opened a new path to reform, as they created a forum in which legal entrepreneurs could challenge discriminatory laws. When international courts and commissions eventually recognized criminalization of homosexuality as an abuse of human rights, they gifted a rhetorical weapon to gay activists.

The two most significant institutional developments were the establishment of the European Court of Human Rights in 1959, and the creation of an individual complaints mechanism under the First Optional Protocol to the International Covenant on Civil and Political Rights in 1976. While there were a number of earlier cases in which the European Court of Human Rights offered some limited support to transsexuals, between 1955 and 1980 the European Commission on Human Rights declared all individual applications concerning criminalization of homosexuality (save one) to be inadmissible. But individuals and groups continued to lodge applications,[7] and in 1981 the European Court of Human Rights upheld a claim by Jeffrey Dudgeon, a Belfast shipping clerk, and ruled that 'the existence of criminal offences relating to homosexual conduct in private between consenting males over the age of 21, or some lesser age, constituted an interference with a person's right to respect for his private life' that contravened Article 8 of the European Convention on Human Rights (1950). This and subsequent decisions (*Norris v. Ireland*, 1988; *Modinos v. Cyprus*, 1993) concerned only European law, but they suggested that human rights legal activism might be successful in other jurisdictions.

Equivalent success outside Europe came in 1994 when Nicholas Toonen made an individual complaint to the UN Human Rights Committee against the criminalization of homosexuality in the Australian state of Tasmania. (The Committee is a body of experts that oversees the International Covenant on Civil and Political Rights.) The Committee found that Australia had breached its obligations to provide 'equality before the law' and non-discrimination on the basis of 'sex' under the International Convention on Civil and Political Rights – the term 'sex' in Article 26 was interpreted as encompassing 'sexual orientation'. The UN Human Rights Committee has no powers of enforcement and its resolutions are commonly ignored, so this decision could easily have been rejected. However, Australia's federal Labor government used the Toonen decision as an opportunity to overrule state laws that criminalized sexual acts between males. (Subsequent Australian federal governments have simply ignored the same Committee's findings on many matters, such as violation of the human rights of asylum seekers.)

In the wake of the Toonen decision, four other UN human rights treaty bodies declared that their treaties should also be interpreted to protect sexual minorities.[8] While these cases established a precedent within the UN and ostensibly created obligations for states to comply, none of the international human rights treaties possess effective enforcement mechanisms. Given that international law normally only applies with the direct consent of those countries affected, and given that the Toonen decision involved an 'activist' judicial reinterpretation of a treaty text, many governments felt entitled to disregard it. Protection of 'sexual orientation' had not been discussed during the negotiation of the Covenant, and opposing countries, including the United States, argued that sexuality should only be protected by human rights instruments with the specific agreement of signatory governments. However, the Toonen decision placed homosexuality firmly on the agenda of human rights questions that were open for international discussion. This is probably most significant in the context of Human Rights bodies' review processes, of which the most prominent is now the UN Human Rights Council's 'Universal Periodic Review'. Since other nations and civil society groups participate in the Council's process, the precedent established by the Toonen case created an unambiguous justification for these stakeholders to raise concerns about violations of queer rights.

In 2006 a meeting of sixteen legal and human rights experts organized by two prominent NGOs (the International Commission of Jurists and the International Service for Human Rights) drafted the 'Yogyakarta Principles on the Application of International Human Rights Law in relation to Sexual Orientation and Gender Identity'.[9] This scrupulously international meeting – held in Indonesia, a country with a Muslim majority, chaired by Sonia Onufer Correa of Brazil and Vitit Muntarbhorn of Thailand, and with a diverse international membership – was a deliberate attempt to codify and promote international legal norms. While these efforts may have catalysed shifts in judicial decision-making, they did not prompt an obvious change in government attitudes.

Regional human rights courts and social change

One reason why international legal developments may have had limited practical impact is that international law has sometimes raced ahead of domestic cultural work; the experience of national- and regional-level legal change suggests that cultural shift must usually be the first step in any successful strategy to expand sexual freedoms. Courts have generally only been willing to recognize human rights protection in the context of growing domestic support. As we have seen, this was the case in Europe, and a similar pattern can be observed in the Inter-American Court of Human Rights' recognition, in the 2012 case *Atala v. Chile*, that discrimination on the basis of sexual orientation is unlawful. In November 2013, the related Inter-American Commission on Human Rights consolidated these changes by creating a 'Rapporteurship on the Rights of Lesbian, Gay, Bisexual, Trans and Intersex Persons (LGBTI)'. Since these developments follow a decade of dramatic cultural change in South America, they are likely to entrench human rights standards in the region further.

In southeast Asia the regional grouping, the Association of Southeast Asian Nations (ASEAN), includes a number of authoritarian nations, some of which (e.g. Malaysia) are vocally hostile to queer rights and most of which are nervous about developing a strong human rights infrastructure. Although an ASEAN Intergovernmental Commission on Human Rights was established in 2009, it is no more than a 'consultative body', and the 2012 ASEAN Human Rights Declaration has been widely critiqued for omitting reference to 'sexual orientation and gender identity'. Nevertheless, Vietnam's move to partial recognition of same-sex marriages, and public statements by some members of the ASEAN

Intergovernmental Commission on Human Rights (e.g. the Indonesian representative), demonstrate that sexual rights are increasingly being debated. During negotiation of the ASEAN Human Rights declaration, Malaysia pushed unsuccessfully to delete protection against discrimination on the bases of 'other status', anticipating that it would be interpreted in accordance with established legal precedent as providing protection for 'sexual orientation and gender identity'. While ASEAN states did not specify sexuality as a subject of protection, in retaining the words 'other status' they knowingly opened the door to judicial decisions protecting sexual orientation and gender identity.[10]

African courts and human rights bodies are also influenced both by developments in international human rights law and by strong domestic opposition to sexuality rights. In 2014 Uganda's highest court struck down that country's anti-homosexuality bill, but sidestepped both national and international controversy by doing so on the basis of a technicality (that the legislation had passed without a quorum), without considering alternative grounds. Regional rights bodies have an equally mixed record. At the time of writing, the African Court on Human and Peoples' Rights has not produced a gay-friendly decision. However, in 2014 the related African Commission on Human and

People's Rights adopted a resolution that condemned violence and discrimination against people on the basis of their sexual orientation and gender identity.[11] While this resolution has no direct legal impact, it boosts the prospects that the regional court might follow international precedents in future decisions. Sociologist Paul Johnson notes that since the preamble to the African Charter on Human and People's rights promises 'to eradicate all forms of colonialism from Africa', the colonial origins of the region's anti-homosexuality laws might potentially be used to undermine them.[12] Certainly this strategy of emphasizing the colonial origins of anti-gay laws is used by many activists.

Regional movements elsewhere are less positive. The Gulf Cooperation Council's announcement in 2013 that it was developing medical tests to stop homosexual and transsexual workers from entering member countries reflects (worrying) official attitudes and the constant risks of persecution facing the region's guest workers. Obviously, the promise of a medical test was an empty boast with no scientific basis.

Feminism and the language of sexual rights

The development of a new language of human rights in the 1970s coincided with the rebirth of feminism as a major force, and the two came together through various national and international processes to create a new concept of 'sexual rights'. There are a number of ways in which this term is used; we understand it to encompass the right to determine and declare one's sexual and gender identity; the uncoerced choice of sexual and marriage partners; protection against all forms of sexual violence; the right to control one's reproductive choices (including abortion); the right to buy and sell sexual services but also to be protected against exploitation and trafficking; the provision of accurate and non-judgemental sexual information and education; protection from sexual harassment etc. We also recognize there will be grey areas, such as legitimate disagreement about appropriate age of consent and the line between sexually positive pornography and images which degrade and encourage violence, and these grey areas will change over time as new norms and technologies develop (most dramatically those that are increasing the possibilities of reproduction through biomedical techniques).

The 1970s momentum towards protection for women's human rights included work on sexual rights, which were initially formulated around questions of reproductive rights and protection against sexual violence, rape and forced sterilization. Following a World Conference in Mexico City to mark International

Women's Year (1975), the UN General Assembly adopted the Convention on Elimination of All Forms of Discrimination Against Women in 1979. While the Convention sought equality for women, it avoided references to violence or to any forms of sexual pleasure or freedoms.

However, sexual rights were raised at a series of large international United Nations Conferences on Human Rights (Vienna 1993), Population and Development (Cairo 1994) and Women (Beijing 1995). At the Beijing Conference activists were ejected from the plenary hall after unfurling a banner that proclaimed: 'Lesbian Rights are Human Rights'. The coalitions of religious and nationalist conservatives against liberal governments and NGOs that battled over women's rights at these conferences are largely the same formations that have been fighting over sexuality rights ever since.

By the time of the 1994 Cairo Conference, international statements were beginning to acknowledge that reproductive rights and sexual health required people to 'have a satisfying and safe sex life', even if the term 'sexual rights' was not employed.[13] The Platform for Action that came out of the 1995 Beijing Conference went further, in recognizing that '[t]he human rights of women include their right to have control over and decide freely and responsibly on matters related to their sexuality, including sexual and reproductive health'. Along with the increasing emphasis in the AIDS world on the links between health and human rights, a new paradigm of 'sexual rights' was being created, one that conservatives were quick to oppose.

While some feminists developed a new language of sexual rights, which meshed well with the discourses around health and human rights promoted by the Global Programme on AIDS and later by the Joint United Nations Programme on HIV/AIDS (UNAIDS), most of the established development NGOs were very slow to bring sexual rights, and particularly gay rights, into their work. One of the first was the Dutch group the Humanist Institute for Cooperation (Hivos) – not surprising, perhaps, as Hivos was established in response to the dominance of religious organizations working in the field of development in the Netherlands – but even Hivos only took up the issue in connection with HIV. Other major secular development NGOs, such as Oxfam and Save the Children, have been slow to take up issues of sexuality, perhaps because their focus has been heavily on poverty elimination.

Established human rights NGOs such as Human Rights Watch moved earlier and added sexuality to their mandates in the early 1990s, following considerable lobbying by gay activists, sometimes working within the organizations. Amnesty International recognized people jailed for advocacy of homosexual rights as prisoners of conscience in 1979, but only recognized those imprisoned for their homosexuality in 1991.[14] During decades of debate opponents noted that sexual orientation was not protected by international human rights law, and that advocacy for homosexuality would undermine Amnesty's support in many parts of the world.[15]

During the 1990s international gay organizations began to support claims for asylum on the grounds of sexual orientation, which was an early focus for IGLHRC.[16] An important turning point came in 2008 when the United Nations High Commissioner for Refugees adopted a 'guidance note on refugee claims relating to sexual orientation and gender identity', and the Organization for Refuge, Asylum and Migration was established to advocate for refugees fleeing brutalization due to sexual orientation or gender identity. There are particular problems associated with establishing refugee status on grounds of sexual/gender identity, summed up in the Organization's phrase as the 'paradox of persecution – where secrecy is crucial for safety, but protection requires revealing identity'.[17] In recipient countries this often means immigration authorities struggle with unfamiliar and culturally sensitive questions, as applicants seek to establish the legitimacy of their claims for asylum. It is not uncommon for applicants to be told to go back to their countries of origin and conceal their sexuality or gender identity, although in 2013 the European Court of Justice followed the High Court of Australia in 2003 and the UK Supreme Court in 2010 by ruling that the option of 'voluntary concealment' in the country of origin was not a valid basis on which to reject an asylum claim. It is very difficult to establish accurate figures on claims for asylum based on sexuality, but anecdotally the most claims have been accepted in Sweden, Canada and the United States.

Recently there have been some attempts to demonstrate a connection between repression of sexual and gender diversity and lack of development, and the World Bank has funded research on the connections between poverty and homophobia. Certainly the marginalization suffered by people perceived to be sexually or gender deviant is likely to have some economic impact, and persecution of sexual minorities clearly has material consequences when it hampers access to health, welfare or educational services. As one report on homosexual men in Ethiopia suggests: 'Breaking away to live out same-sex orientation or rejection after being exposed as gay usually carries enormous social costs, including loss of family status and income.'[18]

HIV, health and human rights

While tentative moves were being made to incorporate sexuality into human rights jurisprudence, the unfolding HIV/AIDS pandemic was connecting human rights and sexuality in other ways. Arresting the spread of HIV required that women have the capacity to refuse unsafe sex, and that MSM and sex workers, as well as injecting drug users, be incorporated within public health campaigns. By the late 1980s public health practitioners and gay activists found common cause in demanding protection of individual sexual rights. Governments that adopted a model of engaging with communities that were most vulnerable to HIV claimed greater public health success than did those who adopted a purely medical 'test and control' response. The lead essay in the first issue of *Health and Human Rights* noted that 'the evolving HIV/AIDS pandemic has shown a consistent pattern through which discrimination, marginalization, stigmatization and, more generally, a lack of respect for the human rights and dignity of individuals and groups heightens their vulnerability to becoming exposed to HIV'.[19] For these authors, who included Jonathan Mann, the founder of the World Health Organization's Global Programme on AIDS, human rights and health were mutually reinforcing.

Responding to HIV/AIDS forced sexuality onto the agendas of a wide range of national and international organizations and turned gay activists into important stakeholders. China's response to HIV illustrates how engaging with HIV can shift official attitudes towards MSM. Since sexuality is not discussed very openly in Chinese society, and homosexual transmission initially played a modest role in China's HIV epidemic, MSM were not initially included in China's first Comprehensive AIDS Response Programme (China CARES) in 2003. However, growing understanding of the epidemic soon prompted the Ministry of Health to propose strategies to involve MSM.[20]

The increasing emphasis on individual rights as against radical social transformation, which is in part a consequence of the collapse of Communism as a viable alternative to capitalism, has benefitted sexual minorities in many parts of the world. In some ways this is a 'politics of recognition' as against that of 'redistribution', and it can dismay those who invoke religion, tradition and culture to preserve what they see as fundamental human institutions. Without suggesting any inevitable linear progress, it is likely that the trend to include sexuality and gender expression in the international language of human rights will continue. It is not necessarily always the case that this will translate to real gains on the ground.

FOUR

The conservative backlash

Crucial to queer movements since the 1970s is the assertion of homosexuality as the basis of an identity, rather than a behaviour that could co-exist within a dominant sexual and gender order. By moving the understanding of sexuality into the public sphere, and creating a new category rather akin to an ethnic minority, this catapulted homosexuality into public debates in a new and not always positive way. Whether around decriminalization, anti-discrimination provisions or same-sex marriage, homosexuality has often become a touchstone for larger cultural wars, and there is a long history of political and religious elites using panic around the spectre of homosexuality to bolster their power. Such backlashes have occurred – seemingly independently – in all regions of the world. In this chapter we examine these responses as they have occurred within national politics, and in the next chapter we contextualize them within an emerging global pattern of polarization over sexuality.

It is important to remember how recent are the shifts in attitudes towards homosexuality in those western countries that are now seeking to impose similar rights elsewhere. The rapidity of change in many countries can give heart to those in other parts of the world struggling for acceptance of sexual and gender diversity. But it is equally probable that these shifts could only occur in societies with a particular mix of affluence, some formal commitment to gender equality and an individualistic political culture. Increasing awareness of gay movements and their victories in western countries seems to have created a strong reaction in other parts of the world, where homosexuality can be mobilized as a way of opposing those aspects of 'globalization' most disliked by powerful elites and feared by many of their more conservative followers. In the formulation of 'Asian Values' in the early 1990s, Singapore's president Lee Kuan Yew and Malaysia's prime minister Mohammed Mahathir singled out acceptance of homosexuality as a product of western hedonism to be avoided: 'Western societies', wrote Mahathir, 'are riddled with single-parent families which foster incest, with homosexuality, with cohabitation … and of course with rejection of religious teachings and values.'[1] Mahathir subsequently used allegations of sodomy to remove and imprison his deputy and rival, Anwar Ibrahim. Meanwhile, Lee Kuan Yew ultimately changed his mind and argued – unsuccessfully – that Singapore needed to decriminalize homosexuality as part of its ambitions to be a global financial centre, while noting that 'If we want creative people then we [have] got to put up with their idiosyncrasies as long so they don't infect the heartland.'[2]

Some of the most striking examples of political homophobia occurred in the former Yugoslavia, where the collapse of a Communist state created a number of nationalist movements, resulting in civil wars and the new (or restored) nations of Serbia, Croatia, Slovenia, Montenegro, Macedonia, Bosnia and Herzegovina, and eventually Kosovo. The complex religious and cultural heritage of the former Yugoslavia includes Catholics, the Orthodox and Muslims, and the state was created after World War I by Serbia, which brought together territories formerly ruled by Austria and Turkey to form the new kingdom. During World War II the country was again divided, and afterwards was held together through the post-war dictatorship of Marshal Tito, who sought to create a sense of Yugoslav nationality.

After Tito's death, separatist movements emerged, leading to the independence first of Slovenia and Croatia, and to a decade of civil warfare in which nationalist and ethnic tensions escalated. During these battles both Croats and Serbs adopted a hyper-masculinist nationalism, which built on ethnic and religious rivalries across most of ex-Yugoslavia. Nationalist rivalries were often reflected both in attitudes towards homosexuality, and in homosexual relationships themselves; Sasho Lambevski has described the combination of repressed desire and ethnic identity between Albanian and Macedonian men seeking sex in the Macedonian capital Skopje, acknowledging the ways national and sexual identities can become interconnected.[3] The Yugoslav wars were the first in contemporary times when male rape was recognized as a major form of violence, and its documentation reminds us that rape is more about the assertion of power than about sexual gratification.[4] In this century the post-war ex-Yugoslav nations have seen the gradual emergence of queer politics, most notably in Croatia and Slovenia, and pressure from the European Union to prohibit discrimination. At the same time embryonic gay movements face considerable opposition, including attacks on gay pride marches in several Balkan countries.

Along with Slovenia, Croatia has become an EU member and sought to become 'European', and its government has therefore wanted to demonstrate a willingness to protect queer groups to avoid condemnation by western governments and NGOs. Serbia, which is far more ambivalent in its attitude towards Europe – and correspondingly more sympathetic to Russia – has been far less willing to change policies despite pressures created by its EU accession process; its prime minister since 2014, Alexsandar Vučić, has made clear his personal dislike of homosexuality and his opposition to pressure from western European sources to protect queer rights.

During the 1990s, the targeting of homosexuality as an unwelcome sign of western cultural colonialism surfaced in a number of countries. Leaders in southern Africa – Mugabe in Zimbabwe; Nujoma in Namibia; Chiluba in Zambia – all attacked homosexuality in extreme rhetoric that was quite different from that of the colonial era. As Mark Gevisser wrote at the end of the century:

> The internet, satellite TV and video rental stores are all key elements in the development of gay consciousness in Africa. But as this happens, nerves become raw, as is clearly evidenced from the anger unleashed in African political and clerical leaders: for the first time, severely repressed societies are forced to talk about sex, a conversation which ends, logically, at a new analysis of gender, and roles that men and women play in both bedroom and society.[5]

While we might take issue with the suggestion that African societies are somehow more 'severely repressed' than others, similar reactions occurred across the globe, including within many western countries themselves. The rise of the Moral Majority in the United States during the 1980s, and Margaret Thatcher's 'Section 28' laws in the UK in 1988, which were aimed at preventing 'the promotion of homosexuality', were in some ways forerunners of what is now occurring globally. George W. Bush made the attack on same-sex marriage central to his successful presidential campaign in 2004, appealing to the fears of conservative religious voters. In France the term 'gender' has unleashed huge anxieties amongst conservatives, who clearly see in the concept the very frightening assumption that what is taken for granted as 'natural' may in fact be a social construct and hence permeable. The planned recognition of same-sex marriage in 2013 led to huge protests, at that point the largest street gatherings in France for several decades.

During this century it appears that visibility and increased repression have sometimes gone hand in hand. In 2001 Egyptian authorities raided a gay party on a Nile River boat, leading to a wave of arrests, beatings, imprisonments and national outcry against homosexuality. While Hosni Mubarak was still in power, homosexuality was already being cast as a spectre of debauchery introduced by external powers, particularly

the United States,[6] and successive Egyptian governments have sought to link homosexuality to opposition
and anti-Egyptian forces. Unconfirmed but steady
reports from Iraq both before and after occupation by
ISIS suggest extrajudicial murder of homosexuals is
not uncommon.

A backlash can occur when there is a perceived shift
in values and policies which unsettles the status quo and
leads to a conservative desire to confront changes they
fear. We accept the argument of Bosia and Weiss that
both identity-based politics and opposition to them are
products of globalization, and that 'It seems that the
all-too-rosy glow of Western leadership in exporting
LGBT rights has rendered the West's equally prominent
role in the diffusion of homophobia nearly invisible.'[7]
Unlike the actions in the United States of the Moral
Majority, who were reacting to perceived gains by a
well-organized gay movement, political homophobia
has emerged in countries without an assertive gay
movement, sometimes spurring a few brave activists to
speak out, encouraged by the new language of sexual
rights and the support of at least some western
governments.

In the period of writing this book there were almost
daily examples of homosexuals being targeted by
both state and religious authorities. During the Ebola

outbreaks in 2014 Liberian religious leaders, including the Council of Churches and the Catholic archbishop Lewis Zeigler, suggested Ebola was God's punishment for acceptance of homosexuality. Predictably, homophobic attacks soared in the following months, and there were reports of growing harassment and police repression in a number of countries in west Africa, including some that had seemed to allow space for vibrant, if small, queer worlds.[8]

In eastern Europe, right-wing parties often adopt homophobic rhetoric as part of a general attack on liberal values, and a nationalistic response to what is perceived as intrusion by European institutions. In Hungary, Jobbik, a party which polled well in European elections in 2014, has echoed Russian calls to criminalize the 'promotion of homosexuality', while Viktor Orbán's government has introduced a new constitution which prohibits gay marriage, as well as a Family Protection Bill. The Russian legislation of 2013 prompted a number of eastern European and central Asian countries to introduce similar bans on 'homosexual propaganda'. In most cases these moves failed to result in legislation, but they suggest the strength of anti-gay feelings amongst at least sections of the population. Again the link between anti-homosexual feelings and a certain sort of nationalism is evident, as in Kyrgyzstan, where one comment suggests the legislation 'may be seen as part of a trend in the country towards the preservation of "traditional values" and Kyrgyz nationalism'. Despite this claim, the same article frames the debate over gay rights as a proxy cultural war between Russia and the United States as each seeks influence in central Asia.[9]

While western European and Latin American states have moved towards abolishing all legal discrimination based on sexuality, there have been shifts in the opposite direction elsewhere. Of course legal neutrality, or even legal protection of rights based on sexual or gender diversity, do not by themselves achieve equality. People still face harassment and violence based on their perceived sexuality in countries that have adopted model laws, and attitudes can often be polarized within countries themselves. There is almost certainly more violence against people seen as 'perverts' in Brazil, Mexico and the United States than in many countries which still retain laws against homosexuality. Often harassment by police will be justified by catch-all laws referring to vagrancy or public decency, as in the Turkish 'Law on Misdemeanors' or the now repealed Venezuelan 'Law of Vagabonds and Crooks'. The real significance of the anti-gay laws in Russia over the past few years has been the apparent signal they have sent to hooligan attacks on those perceived as gay, and to police to ignore such attacks.

At the same time, there are parts of the world where old laws have been retained, and in some cases strengthened and, more significantly, used as licence for violence and persecution. In Senegal, where the law had criminalized homosexual activity but rarely been applied, there has been a marked increase in police and local anti-gay activities over the past few years. (The Senegalese law was based on what is known as the Mirguet amendment to a 1960 French law which targeted homosexuality as 'a social evil' [*fléau sociale*] – but which was repealed twenty years later.) Since 2008 there has been what one observer termed 'an unprecedented homophobic wave', fed by mass media and certain fundamentalist preachers.[10] Similarly to incidents elsewhere, this particular panic was sparked by reports of an alleged homosexual wedding reported in the popular journal *Icone*. When President Obama visited Dakar in 2012 he called for greater tolerance, but President Macky Sall responded that Senegal was 'not yet ready' to decriminalize homosexuality. This statement was widely reported in the Senegalese media as a show of courage by the country's leader. Presumably neither leader was aware of the fact that in the 1970s gay travel magazines proclaimed Senegal to be 'tolerant about almost everything', and a gay sexual paradise.[11]

A conservative international?

President Sall's response is at least in part linked to a revival of religious fundamentalism in Senegal, in this case Islamic. But similar tendencies are linked to the spread of fundamentalist Christianity, and in more restricted areas Hinduism and Judaism, neither of which is globally evangelical. Currently there is some weakening of state support for sexual diversity in Brazil, linked to the rapid growth in influence of Pentecostalism, which is significant because Brazil was long seen as a global pacesetter in its approach to sexuality within HIV prevention programmes.

Just as support for sexual rights is being globalized, and supported by a number of western-based NGOs, so too homophobia is also being globalized, usually through religious-based organizations. While the Catholic Church under Pope Francis has moderated its language on homosexuality, this is a shift in emphasis rather than doctrine: Francis's predecessor, Benedict XVI, saw homosexuality as 'an objective disorder', and those views are still upheld by a majority of Catholic bishops and dioceses. Wherever it has significant influence the Church has campaigned vigorously to prohibit same-sex marriage and adoption, and Ireland's historic popular vote for same-sex marriage in May 2015 reflects the Church's weakening grip on society, rather than a new openness in the Church. (Catholicism's influence was stronger in Austria, and there, a few weeks after the Irish vote, the national assembly voted strongly against 'marriage equality'.) Homosexuality has long divided the global Anglican movement, with continuing and very bitter battles between those congregations, predominantly in the rich world, which accept same-sex relationships, and their opponents, often based in African dioceses. Indeed there is an ongoing possibility that the divide around homosexuality could catalyse a split in the Anglican Church, with more progressive congregations pressing for acceptance of same-sex marriage and of openly homosexual priests.

The growth of evangelical Christianity and fundamentalist Islam and Hinduism in many parts of the world means that polarization around sexual rights is unlikely to diminish soon. What Clifford Bob terms the 'Baptist–Burqua network' includes the fundamentalist strands of almost all major religions, which can form bizarre alliances in their eagerness to oppose sexual rights.[12]

International organizing to oppose gay rights – and, more broadly, anything that suggests the blurring of gender lines or acceptance of sexual diversity – has paralleled the growth of international gay organizing. American-based organizations defending 'family values' have been particularly active in promoting an anti-homosexual line both in international fora and within a number of overseas countries. Since 1997 the World Congress of Families, a grouping of a number of right-wing religious organizations, has heavily promoted 'traditional family values' through international conferences and support for anti-homosexual groups around the world. They have built strong alliances with religious groups in Russia, particularly with those legislators and clergy who have been promoting anti-homosexual laws. 'The Russians', according to Larry Jacobs of the Congress, 'might be the Christian saviours of the world.'[13]

The development of homophobic rhetoric and legislation in Uganda is often linked to the work of American pastor Scott Lively, a born-again Christian who has campaigned against abortion and homosexuality through a number of US-based organizations. In 2009 Lively was brought to Uganda by local evangelists, and used the opportunity to encourage official homophobia, resulting in the first draft of the anti-homosexuality bill. How far Lively is responsible for this and subsequent bills is unclear, but in 2012 he was sued in the US Federal Court by Sexual Minorities Uganda for encouraging persecution and 'crimes against humanity'; at the time of writing, several courts have upheld the constitutionality of the charges and he faces trial. The use of American law to limit the activities of anti-gay activists overseas is likely to be contested through a number of legal channels, and suggests new steps towards using the legal system within western countries to limit global homophobic networks.

The increasing visibility of queer issues in the past decade has been a fulcrum for religious and nationalist responses, sometimes in the absence of a gay move-ment. Allegations of western-funded queer activism have sparked protests in many countries, and are a constant trope in the rhetoric of many authoritarian leaders. The Ugandan law has been taken up elsewhere in Africa, usually by dictatorships that have clearly found political homophobia a particularly useful way of rallying support. President Yahya Jammeh of the Gambia is known for his brutality towards human rights activists and for his anti-gay rhetoric, having said gays can either leave the country or be executed. In other cases homosexual acts have been criminalized, almost inadvertently, as part of the adoption of sharia law.

In 2014 the oil-rich southeast Asian Sultanate of Brunei adopted sharia law, which provides for stoning to death for homosexual activity. The sultan's move does not appear to have been prompted by homophobia, but rather by his desire to shed his youthful party-boy image and show solidarity with international Islam. This change is likely to have more immediate consequences for women than for homosexuals. Imposition of sharia law in the Aceh province of Indonesia provides for public caning for homosexual activity between both women and men, although at the time of writing there were no known cases of this law being implemented. Aceh, on the western tip of Sumatra, is the most Islamic part of Indonesia, and won special legal status as part of a post-civil-war settlement, so it is unlikely that other parts of Indonesia will follow suit. Currently there are pressures to introduce sharia law in the northern Malaysian state of Kelantan.

It is difficult to separate the idea of an 'LGBT' identity or community from a particular set of individualistic values that are not necessarily shared beyond western liberal societies, and we recognize that the language of activism has helped promote a backlash. Above all, the emphasis on same-sex marriage has become a touchstone for unease in many parts of the world, including some of the countries which have accepted it legally. In cultures which recognize sexual diversity without a sense of homosexuality as a legitimate identity, the idea of two women or men marrying can seem an affront to very deeply held views of how women and men should organize their lives, and has allowed both religious and political elites to build support around claims of protecting traditional values. Marriage was the trigger for anti-homosexual moves in both Uganda and Nigeria; more recently Slovakia, Croatia and the Dominican Republic have sought to 'protect' heterosexual marriage through Constitutional amendments. (In the case of Croatia this was accompanied by the recognition of 'life partnerships' for same-sex couples.)

It is important to recognize that hostility to homosexuality is not merely the product of religious and political leaders, but that they often reflect and are articulating deeply held prejudices within their societies. There is surprisingly little agreement as to just why homosexuality is so widely feared and disliked, although it does seem related to rigid views of gender, in particular to fears that homosexuality somehow undermines masculinity; in the case of men by behaving 'like women', in the case of women by denying the need for men both to enjoy and to dispense sexual pleasure. R. W. Connell's concept of 'hegemonic masculinity', aimed at preserving the dominance of men over women, is important; as Connell writes: 'the contempt for homosexuality and homosexual men...is part of the ideological package of hegemonic masculinity'.[14] Opposition to sexual diversity combines both consciously political and unconscious fears and desires, which makes countering it particularly difficult.

What appears to unite most of the opponents to gay rights is the desire to preserve a particular sort of gender regime, in which there is a clear distinction between women and men, and an assumption that children can only thrive within a heterosexual family. Defence of children is integral to much anti-homosexual rhetoric, whether it be to prevent 'recruiting' through sex education or to oppose same-sex parents, a major theme in resistance to gay marriage. Any strategy to expand acceptance of sexual diversity needs to recognize these fears, however invalid they might appear, and counter them.

Inevitably the stress on the most obvious examples of persecution means that it is easy to overlook the myriad of subtle ways in which discrimination continues, and that many homosexuals internalize this discrimination in ways that restrict them in living fulfilling lives. Again, there is a growing gap between those parts of the world where discrimination against people based on their sexuality or gender expression is officially discouraged, and those where sexual diversity is actively discouraged and penalized.

As anti-discrimination laws and same-sex marriage become accepted in many western countries, there is a renewed focus on institutions other than the state, and their role in promoting sexual conformity. There have been highly publicized cases in both the United States and Great Britain revolving around the right of individual businesses to deny services to people because of their sexuality, often justified as a defence of religious freedom. Increasingly the mainstream gay movement is focusing on business, and the need for the private sector to develop active policies of non-discrimination even where this is not required by law. Economic globalization certainly creates opportunities for activists to press global firms to adopt non-discriminatory practices in all jurisdictions, and in many parts of the world this may well prove a more effective means of changing attitudes than relying on government action. Pressure for queer equality in rich nations may effectively lead to multinational corporations taking the lead internationally in situations where government authorities and religious leaders are hostile.

FIVE

International polarization

As the successes of the gay rights movement in some places have been mirrored by increasing homophobic repression in others, the result has been growing international polarization. Social, legal and intellectual changes starting in the 1960s ultimately created circumstances in which some governments began to argue that discrimination on the basis of 'sexual orientation and gender identity' was a violation of universal human rights. In response, other states proposed an alternative norm: that human rights are only valid if they are grounded in the 'universal traditional values of mankind' – from the perspective of traditional morality, homosexuality is a social vice and sin which may be criminalized. Whereas only a few decades ago sexuality went unmentioned in global institutions, today sexual rights are the subject of heated international debate.

The theatrics of international politics – such as the moment in March 2012 when almost half the national representatives walked out of the UN Human Rights Council, as it began to discuss a report on sexual-orientation-based discrimination – are of largely symbolic importance. The international posturing of governments doesn't always reflect domestic practices, and there is often a gap between the polarized debates in human rights bodies and the practical work of some UN agencies. Likewise, while laws governing homosexuality are important, in many cases they do not reflect the reality of gay experience. Today, homosexual acts are lawful in Russia but illegal in Singapore, yet Singapore is home to a flourishing gay scene and political movement that – unlike in Russia – is largely free from official or unofficial harassment. Yet while international human rights debates and legal trends do not determine the dynamics of persecution and acceptance that affect the lives of ordinary people, neither are they wholly disconnected. Regional and international dynamics have repercussions for queer rights on the ground, even if the interconnections between national politics and global trends are often complex.

Regional and international politics

There are clear patterns in the formal responses of governments to questions of sexuality that align with international regional and religious groupings. The majority of countries that retain criminal sanctions against homosexual behaviour are members of either the Commonwealth or the Organisation of Islamic Cooperation (OIC), or both. While the Commonwealth is a loose organization of some fifty-five countries, almost all of them former British colonies, it has no means of enforcing norms other than through expulsion of member nations, a move which began with the expulsion of South Africa in 1961 for its policies of apartheid, and continued with more recent expulsions of several countries for their lack of democracy.

The Commonwealth Charter claims that its members are united in support of democracy, human rights and the rule of law, and demands for recognizing sexuality as included within the human rights penumbra have become significant. An Eminent Persons Group, established in 2011, recommended that existing criminal sanctions against homosexuality should be removed, in part because of their impact on effective HIV prevention. But while a meeting of Commonwealth foreign ministers adopted the recommendation for a human rights charter in 2012, Commonwealth member countries have been amongst those most active in increasing legal penalties against homosexuality in the past few years. It seems very unlikely that the Commonwealth will be a major avenue for pursuing sexual rights in the foreseeable future.[1]

Another regional approach has responded to international debates about human rights and gender identity in a more distinctive way. Pakistan's highest court recognized the status of a third gender (*hijra*) in 2009. This traditional accommodation of gender non-conformity may be viewed as an indirect response to international legal debates over 'sexual orientation and gender identity' – the court accepted protection of a gender identity that reflected local traditions, but has not accepted the case for decriminalization of homosexual acts.[2] In 2014 the Indian Supreme Court reached a similar decision when it extended legal recognition to transgendered people, and referred to a raft of international precedents – including the Yogyakarta Principles and the Pakistani case – in reaching this decision. A distinct regional norm seems to have emerged in south Asia, with legal recognition of a 'third gender' category in Pakistan, Nepal, Bangladesh and India.

Meanwhile, most of 'Confucian' Asia has remained largely uninvolved in the international dispute over gay rights. While some governments, such as that of China, typically vote in opposition to sexuality rights internationally, there has been no obvious move towards increased domestic repression of sexual minorities or efforts to exploit the issue for political gain. Other states, such as Vietnam, have indicated partial acceptance of same-sex identities, but have not promoted this norm internationally, which is consistent with their opposition to any interference in the 'internal affairs' of other countries.

Russia under Putin has emerged as a powerful leader in anti-homosexual rhetoric, both domestically and internationally. While homophobic public rhetoric is common and has been used to solidify links between Putin's regime and the Russian Orthodox Church, homosexual sex has been decriminalized since 1993. However, a more recent agreement between Putin and the Russian Orthodox Church gives the Church a particular role in reviewing possible legislation, and the Church has played an official role in promoting social conservatism.

Russia's homophobic rhetoric is part of a sophisticated international public diplomacy campaign, which seeks to narrow the validity of human rights to those that are consistent with 'universal traditional values'. Through this explicit rejection of sexuality rights, Putin has sought to form international alliances with those who critique secular human rights from religious or collectivist traditions, and to encourage allies to use the issue of sexual rights to distinguish themselves from the west. In a 2013 speech Putin argued:

> Today, many nations are revising their moral values and ethical norms, eroding ethnic traditions and differences between peoples and cultures. Society is now required not only to recognise everyone's right to the freedom of consciousness, political views and privacy, but also to accept without question the equality of good and evil...We know that there are more and more people in the world who support our position on defending traditional values that have made up the spiritual and moral foundation of civilization in every nation for thousands of years: the values of traditional families, real human life, including religious life, not just material existence but also spirituality, the values of humanism and global diversity.[3]

Putin's allies have used a 'civilizational critique' of human rights to marginalize domestic liberal opponents, to consolidate the Orthodox Church's support for the Kremlin, to blunt the domestic impact of western critiques of Putin's human rights record, and as an instrument of Russian soft power internationally.[4] Allying with both Islamic and Christian opponents of gay rights adds to Russia's credibility in many parts of the world, and helps define it as representing an alternative to western values.

Polarization

When new norms are proposed internationally, some states will typically defend the status quo by clarifying and formalizing their opposition. When the international community began to condemn apartheid in 1946, the South African government asserted the principle of non-interference in internal affairs and adopted laws that codified racial discrimination.[5] While disputation over apartheid continued for several decades, in this case the new norm of racial equality ultimately won widespread international acceptance. Female enfranchisement and prohibition of slavery are other examples of norms that have been adopted globally after initial resistance, even if they continue to be violated in practice – such as the tolerance for slavery in Mauritania. Despite these hopeful precedents, global acceptance of gay rights is not similarly inevitable: ongoing polarization is also possible, as is true of whaling and the death penalty. As in the case of whaling, discussion of sexuality is complicated by claims that national identity and traditions are being compromised by cultural imperialism.

Once some countries and human rights bodies accepted that human rights protect sexual minorities, it was inevitable that other countries would disagree, but it was not inevitable that the debate should become as polarized as it now appears. The dispute over whether human rights protection should cover 'sexual orientation and gender identity' has become so fractious that it has created an opportunity for Russia and the OIC to undermine the wider concept of secular human rights, and has frustrated the work of some UN bodies. Thus in 2010 the UN General Assembly rejected an otherwise innocuous report from the Special Rapporteur on education because it supported access to 'comprehensive sexual education' – conservative governments worried that such education might normalize sexual diversity.

The story of international disputation over homosexuality begins with the development of LGBT-specific international organizations. The International Lesbian and Gay Association (ILGA) was granted official consultative status with the United Nations Economic and Social Council in 1993.[6] However, conservative US Senator Jesse Helms revealed historical links between several of ILGA's member organizations and paedophile groups, as part of a campaign to overturn this decision. (Although ILGA itself refused to admit paedophile groups, it was unable to guarantee that no member organization has continuing links.) Helms persuaded the US Senate to make withdrawing ILGA's recognition a precondition for payment of the US's $118-million debt to the UN, and ILGA's consultative status was suspended for several years. Nevertheless, LGBT organizations were officially accredited at both the 1993 World Conference on Human Rights and the 1995 Fourth World Conference on Women in Beijing, and in time such representation has become commonplace.

In 1999, Asma Jahangir, the UN Special Rapporteur on extrajudicial executions, submitted a report to the UN Commission on Human Rights which argued that imposition of the death penalty for sexuality-related offences breached the Covenant on Civil and Political Rights' guarantee of a 'right to life'. Jahangir called for universal decriminalization and drew attention to extrajudicial killings of homosexuals in Brazil, Colombia and Mexico.[7] At first, the international community reacted to Jahangir's report in a reasonable and routine manner, and added specific reference to killings on the basis of 'sexual orientation' to a regular resolution condemning extrajudicial killings. However, over the following decade, while resolutions mentioning sexual orientation continued to pass, each vote was fiercely contested and the anti-gay camp gained strength. Finally, in November 2010, a motion sponsored by Benin deleted any reference to 'sexual orientation' from the resolution.[8]

This was not the first time that opponents of sexual rights had scored an important victory – however, it was the first such victory secured without the approval of the United States. In 2003, Brazil had introduced a broad draft resolution titled 'Human Rights and Sexual Orientation' to the UN Commission on Human Rights. Strong resistance delayed an initial vote and Brazil eventually requested a permanent postponement. Discussion of the Brazilian resolution exposed deep divisions among governments, and opposition from members of the OIC was particularly strong.[9] Since the Bush Administration was also opposed (it planned to abstain rather than vote against), the Brazilian proposal was clearly untenable.[10] For so long as the United States sided with the conservatives, international debate over sexuality rights was contained. Despite significant international disagreement, there would be no serious challenge to the status quo while an informal alliance existed between the world's only superpower and a network of conservative developing states.

Election of the Obama Administration shifted this balance. After the defeat of the resolution condemning extrajudicial killings on the basis of 'sexual orientation', the United States ambassador to the UN, Susan Rice, sponsored an alternative resolution, and the General Assembly reversed the earlier decision (by a vote of ninety-three to fifty-five, with twenty-seven abstentions). The UN African Group and the OIC are usually staunch opponents of sexual rights; however, in response to US pressure, the unity of the African Group was broken, and South Africa, Angola, Cape Verde and Rwanda were among the countries persuaded to vote for the resolution.[11]

Under Obama the United States took an increasingly activist position on international gay rights, responding to growing interest and pressure from domestic organizations which make up a significant constituency for the Democratic Party. Without casting doubt on Obama's genuine commitment, statements by high-level US government officials sometimes appear directed more at domestic voters than at persuading the countries which are under scrutiny. In 2015, the United States appointed a Special Envoy for the Human Rights of LGBT Persons, and Obama has increasingly referred to this issue in his speeches. Disagreement with President

Kenyatta over gay rights was a prominent theme in Obama's visit to Kenya in July 2015.

In 2011, the US was instrumental in a resolution of the UN Human Rights Council instructing the High Commissioner for Human Rights to prepare a report on 'discriminatory laws and practices... against individuals based on their sexual orientation and gender identity, and how international human rights law' could provide redress.[12] Whereas the earlier Brazilian resolution suffered from a lack of coordination among supportive states and NGOs, this new resolution was carefully planned. Voting (twenty-three in favour, nineteen against, three abstentions) again saw strong opposition from the OIC and the African Group. However, in order to avoid the impression of western neo-colonialism, South Africa was chosen to present the final text.

The year 2011 was also when the US State Department founded a $3-million Global Equality Fund 'to support programs that advance the human rights of lesbian, gay, bisexual and transgender (LGBT) persons around the world', and also an 'LGBT Core Group' at the United Nations. The LGBT Core Group was a coalition of countries 'committed to eliminating violence and discrimination against individuals based on their sexual orientation and gender identity' and to recognizing that LGBT individuals should enjoy human rights protection. Some members of the LGBT Core Group – such as Japan and Israel – have no previous record of advocacy for sexuality rights either domestically or internationally, so one wonders if their participation might be explained by close alliances with the United States.

Over the past few years both European and US governments have increasingly raised the profile of sexual rights. Thus a ministerial declaration from France, Italy and Belgium in 2013 deliberately linked these rights to the idea of a European identity: 'We want to live in a European space in which individual freedoms are effectively protected, regardless of one's sexual orientation or gender identity'; and groups such as ILGA-Europe have consciously linked themselves to the European project.[13] When Malta voted to accept same-sex civil unions and adoptions in 2014, it boasted that this made it 'more liberal and more European'. UN secretary general Ban Ki-moon has also begun to assert the need for universal recognition of sexual rights, and in 2013, the UN Human Rights Office launched a 'Free & Equal' campaign. Gay rights are simultaneously being promoted in unprecedented ways and assimilated into the legitimating narratives of global power structures.

Conditionality

Conditionality refers to linking conditions to the provision of benefits such as loans or aid. The post-World War II Marshall Plan required 'participating countries' to adopt 'self-help measures' that supported free trade (especially with the United States) and currency convertibility, while throughout its history the International Monetary Fund (IMF) has sought to link funding to policy measures. Since conditionality's purpose is to promote a donor's goals, it intentionally restricts recipients' autonomy, and this exploitation of power differentials is frequently controversial. On the other hand, untied aid creates perverse incentives for rulers, since an impoverished population may attract aid flows that can be diverted to empower ruling elites and undermining democratizing reforms.[14] These dilemmas might potentially be resolved through carefully designed conditionality, such as grassroots participation and ownership of aid projects, and an insistence that programmes promote gender equality. However, evidence suggests that conditionality is usually a blunt instrument, since donors struggle to create incentives that allow their goals to take precedence over those of recipients.[15]

During the 1980s, when high interest rates had created crippling balance-of-payments crises in many heavily indebted countries, increasingly strict 'conditionalities' were imposed by the western-dominated IMF and World Bank in exchange for finance. Structural adjustment lending sought to refashion developing economies according to the dictates of liberal economic thinking: reducing the economic role of the state in favour of markets. While economic impacts were mixed, in many cases these policies, which included winding back public health and education services, harmed the poor. The IMF also lost much prestige when those nations that resisted its policy prescriptions recovered fastest from the 1997 Asian financial crisis (Malaysia is the key example). Where the first generation of conditionality focused on neo-liberal economic reform, a second wave promoted a broader liberal agenda around 'good governance' and respect for 'human rights'. Once again, the practical impact of this well-intentioned conditionality was mixed at best.

While aid conditionality has always been controversial, the period in which neoliberal policies (often termed the 'Washington Consensus') were imposed on developing countries has created a significant legacy of distrust. Conditionality that withdraws aid from states which torture or kill those perceived as sexual deviants might seem far removed from IMF demands for governments to charge impoverished children school fees. However, all forms of conditionality seek to impose a donor's agenda and so are likely to trigger a backlash among those on whom 'conditions' are placed. While it seems likely that well-designed 'conditions' might offset the negative dimensions of aid-giving, the very fact that conditionality exploits the north–south power inequality means that it is an imperfect method by which to protect marginalized communities.

International development assistance

Beginning with tentative steps by Sweden and the Netherlands, donor governments over the past decade have sought to find ways to encourage groups working around sexual and gender diversity, often through programmes for HIV prevention. (The Australian government funded a few such groups in the late 1980s, and helped contribute to the emergence of gay networks in southeast Asia.) The first few years of this century saw a strong emphasis on international efforts to combat the spread of HIV and AIDS, and to roll out effective treatments, and AIDS was specifically named, along with malaria and tuberculosis, as a focus of the Millennium Development Goals. While services directed at marginalized groups such as trans* and MSM remain underresourced, the emphasis on HIV and AIDS meant new opportunities for both activists and sympathetic donors to increase their attention to issues of sexuality.

While much of the focus of gay advocacy has been on resolutions by the Human Rights Committee and other parts of the UN system, there has been increasing programmatic activity by some of the United Nations agencies around sexual rights. The creation of UNAIDS in 1996 in order to coordinate the work of all UN agencies around HIV meant an agency whose guiding principles would take up the ideas of health and human rights, and give many LGBT groups access to decision-making. Other UN agencies started to adopt policies and programmes working with diverse sexual and gender minorities; while the United Nations Development Programme took the lead, there are examples now across the UN system of such activities.

As donor governments pledged considerable funds to combat HIV, assistance came with conditions not always acceptable to recipient countries. The clearest case was George W. Bush's very ambitious President's Emergency Plan for AIDS Relief, which funded both treatment and prevention programmes. However, the funding was conditional on accepting certain principles, especially a refusal to support groups working with sex workers, which led Brazil to refuse the funding. The Bush Administration also lined up with conservative governments in various UN resolutions in refusing to name MSM as particularly vulnerable to HIV infection.

The Global Fund to Fight AIDS, Tuberculosis and Malaria was founded in 2002 as a partnership between governments, civil society, the private sector and people affected by the diseases, and has sought to link funding to governments' demonstrating that they are willing to work effectively with marginalized populations most vulnerable to HIV, usually identified as MSM, injecting drug users and sex workers. At the same time, various parts of the United Nations system have taken up issues of sexuality orientation and gender identity, with the support of the secretary general. Regional offices of UNESCO have conducted workshops on homophobia, and UNICEF has committed itself to 'Eliminating discrimination against children and parents based on sexual orientation and/or gender identity', a position that was strongly condemned by some religious groups.[16] At country level, often under pressure from determined staffers, many of the UN agencies have been able to provide resources and support to emerging queer groups, which in turn creates a constituency to continue this work. Perhaps most significantly, the World Bank has pressured loan recipients to halt discrimination against people based on their sexuality and gender identity.

Donor nations, particularly the western Europeans and the United States, have increasingly raised sexual rights generally, and LGBT issues specifically, as part of their general approach to international development.[17] In 2010 the renegotiation of the Cotonou Agreement, which covers trade and political relations between the European Union and seventy-nine African, Caribbean and Pacific nations, became acrimonious when the

European Parliament demanded that 'actions conducted under the terms of the various partnerships be pursued without any discrimination on grounds of gender...sexual orientation or against people living with HIV/AIDS'.[18] African, Caribbean and Pacific states unanimously rejected this threat and wrote a statement which demanded that the European Union 'refrain from any attempts to impose its values' concerning the 'phenomenon of homosexuality'.[19] Next, controversy erupted over the incident described in chapter 1, when UK prime minister David Cameron raised the possibility of withdrawing bilateral aid if African countries increased criminal penalties for homosexuality. Again, targeted governments were furious and the threat appeared to backfire; Malawian politicians at one point blamed LGBT activists for British aid cuts that were wholly unrelated to gay rights. Moreover, critics pointed out that Cameron's announcement was not followed by specific policy descriptions – suggesting that it might have been motivated by domestic political concerns.[20]

A group of African social justice activists responded: 'An effective response to the violations of the rights of LBGTI people has to be more nuanced than the mere imposition of donor sanctions. The history of colonialism and sexuality cannot be overlooked when seeking solutions to this issue.' Sanctions 'sustain the divide between the LGBTI and the broader civil society movement', 'disregard the agency of African civil society' and 'are by their nature coercive and reinforce the disproportionate power dynamics between donor countries and recipients'. The activists went on to call on the UK to abandon aid conditionality, to support 'national and regional human rights mechanisms' and to expand support for community-based and -led LGBTI programmes.[21]

As we have noted, the major shift in US policies under the Obama Administration has served to make this issue far more central to international debates. Comments by President Obama urging various states to decriminalize homosexuality, and the responses to anti-gay laws in countries such as Uganda, have drawn defensive responses from target countries and in some cases have led to increased persecution. The US State Department's resourcing of SOGI-linked civil society groups has also been controversial: when the US Embassy in Pakistan hosted an event honouring 'gays and lesbians', the Lahore High Court Bar Association condemned this as a 'drone attack on culture and social life of the region'.[22]

Since the advent of the Obama Administration, countries that support gay rights have built a powerful alliance and are now usually able to pass resolutions in international fora. But even if there are rhetorical gains, the realities of global division persist. Opponents of gay rights continue to make similar claims: that liberal treatment of sexuality violates religious traditions and national values, and will lead to family and social breakdown. Sexual minorities continue to be targets of violence and political scapegoating across much of the world. In many cases, efforts to promote or impose gay rights have seemed to play into the hands of oppressive governments. The reality of international polarization and the sensitivities about western imperialism in those countries that have only recently escaped colonial domination raise a real question for activists: how best to promote human rights and liberation within a divided world.

SIX

What is to be done?

Hillary Clinton's landmark 2011 speech promising 'LGBT people' threatened by oppressive regimes that 'you have an ally in the United States of America' places those of us who do not meet traditional sexual and gender expectations in an unfamiliar position. We, who were for so long cast as internal enemies, are now rehabilitated as icons of western progressive modernity. Where colonialism was once partially justified as a civilizing response to sexual permissiveness, now protection of vulnerable developing-world queers warrants further western interference. While this reversal is welcome, it also creates profound strategic and ethical dilemmas. Is it possible for outsiders (be they governments or activists) to promote acceptance of sexual diversity in communities of which they are not members? Is it justifiable to seek to impose 'gay rights' on countries that reject them? And if international intervention is justified, what kinds of political strategies might most effectively promote sustainable social change? How should we best promote acceptance of sexual diversity at home and around the world?

Unfortunately, there are no simple answers to these questions, and any effective international engagement must be nuanced, case-specific and aware of the limited capacity that outsiders have to intervene in any community. If we value pluralism and the political autonomy of communities that are still recovering from the injustices of colonialism, we should also be wary of any attempt to impose western standards. On the other hand, complete isolation is neither possible nor desirable. The rhetoric and strategies of political homophobia employed by oppressive governments are just as influenced by global images and networks as are queer politics and notions of 'LGBT' identity. Repressive elites that exploit post-colonial resentments as part of their persecution of homosexuals are supported by a reactionary international network of states and civil society actors. If international politics plays a role in constructing homophobic repression, surely it should also play a role in responding to it? Where authorities torture suspected homosexuals, tolerate corrective rape and honour killings, or implicitly support savage vigilante attacks, can the international community play a useful role?

We approach these difficult questions with three starting intuitions. First, whatever the limitations of 'human rights' as an emancipatory political agenda, the current rhetorical prominence of 'human rights' creates opportunities for the expansion of personal freedoms. Moreover, oppressed people increasingly use the language of human rights and use human rights mechanisms to seek international support in national struggles. Second, we anticipate that lasting social progress can ultimately only emerge from within societies; outsiders might nurture progressive tendencies through engagement and dialogue, but we anticipate that coercion (economic or military) and moralizing will tend to be counterproductive. Third, we suspect that gay liberation will not follow a predetermined trajectory in which each country has a 'Stonewall moment', creates gay districts and eventually legalizes gay marriage. Thus it is possible to imagine a Confucian model of tolerance developing in east Asia, in which sexual diversity and bodily autonomy are protected without homosexuality forming a basis for a master identity. In many societies the extended family is central, and negotiating one's sexuality with one's biological family is the central preoccupation for most people; as Parmesh Shahani wrote in his book *Gay Bombay*: 'Insofar as one's primary community is concerned, the blood family still rules the roost.'[1] The western concept of 'coming out' as the essential ingredient of liberation may not have the same meaning in societies where there are different notions of kinship and community, and is a further reason for scepticism about the constant invocation of 'LGBT community'.[2]

These intuitions lead us to advocate a comparatively modest agenda. If the international system were able to protect people from violence and persecution, this would create space for local activists to push for a deeper acceptance of diverse sexualities, kinships and families. The forms of liberation they pursue may be unfamiliar to us; indeed, some western activists may regard them as 'liberation-lite'. Since international campaigners are likely to misunderstand the kinds of changes that will gain local acceptance, the international effort should focus on universal protection against criminalization and violations of personal safety. If international consensus can be built around these minimal protections, this will support more transformative local changes without dictating them.

The sorry history of colonialism, of 'conditionality' in the post-colonial era, and of invasions and military interventions cloaked in humanitarian ideals should prompt scepticism about promises to protect gay rights internationally. As Malawian academic and activist

Jessie Kabwila has noted: 'Given what usually happens to Malawians and Africans when they follow the lead of the Western-driven international world, asking Malawians to make a paradigmatic attitudinal change on an issue on the basis of what is happening internationally is unwise, wrong and dangerous.'[3]

Of course, not all forms of international influence are counterproductive or coercive. The judgements of the European Court of Human Rights prohibiting criminalization of same-sex sexual activity motivated reform in post-Communist countries seeking to join the Council of Europe after 1989. Similarly, the protection of 'sexual orientation' in European Union Directive 2000/78/EC, and the political requirement that countries must adopt anti-discrimination laws complying with the Directive before they can be considered as candidates for accession to the European Union, have created an expanding zone of progressive law-making. Although the EU's accession requirements can be viewed as a form of conditionality, queer rights have been promoted with carrots rather than imposed with sticks. It seems likely that the voluntary nature of accession-linked conditionality also accounts for its effectiveness: changes are more likely to be accepted if they are perceived as freely and democratically chosen.

Can the international community promote human rights compliance?

Is it possible for the international community to promote human rights compliance where culture, religion and tradition are mobilized against acceptance? Too often this question is asked by westerners without sufficient reflection on their own histories. This book is written by two people from Australia, one of whom has spent sections of his adult life in the US – countries whose race relations have long been the subject of international critique and which, in the decade following September 11, 2001, have seen draconian measures against suspected terrorists and asylum seekers.

Abuses in Australia and the United States have been highlighted by a wide variety of UN human rights bodies, such as the UN Committee Against Torture and the UN Human Rights Committee. However, while both governments were aware of their international legal obligations (the US Department of Justice and the Defense Department produced numerous legal memos to justify the Bush Administration's use of torture), both largely discounted international criticism.

While there has been considerable debate and disquiet in both countries around these policies, politicians have found political rewards in defying international human rights critiques and scapegoating suspected terrorists and asylum seekers, often based on simplistic racial profiles. One Australian federal election was won under the slogan 'We will decide who comes to this country and the manner in which they come.' It is doubtful if any international pressure could have persuaded governments to change these policies. Where change has occurred, as through President Obama's 2009 Executive Order ensuring lawful interrogations, it has been the product of domestic political debates. Domestic human rights defenders are nurtured by international networks, but it is arguments referencing national interests, such as claims that torture is ineffective for intelligence gathering and is a violation of American values, that tend to be effective.

External pressure to promote human rights is likely to be even less effective where there is deep international disagreement and ongoing debate over the content of human rights, as is the case in debates over capital punishment, criminalization of adultery, recognition of polygamous marriage and protection of sexual freedom. Sometimes these debates influence domestic practice; however, these cases also demonstrate the difficulty of shaming a government into compliance with a rights standard it has never accepted. The European Union's condemnation of capital punishment and ban on exports of lethal injection drugs to the United States is occurring at a time when US opinion is turning against the death penalty, so it may seem an exception to this rule. However, being deprived of lethal injection drugs has led some US states to adopt older execution methods, such as by firing squad, and moves to restrict the death penalty are shaped by shifting public opinion and judicial attitudes. (US Supreme Court decisions have taken account of shifts in international law, and Justice Anthony Kennedy, often the key swing vote on social issues, has cited foreign tribunals in decisions on gay rights.) While international human rights standards clearly influence national policy and domestic political debates, international condemnation is rarely an effective way to advance rights protection within western democracies. We see no reason to assume that international pressures will be better received elsewhere.

What's the point of human rights, then?

What is the value of human rights if the international community cannot police them? According to one influential philosophical account, human rights are a set of pre-political entitlements that all people possess simply by virtue of being human. No matter whether these entitlements are viewed as deriving from God or human reason, this view holds that human rights belong to everyone everywhere. In this view human rights are a kind of moral trump card. Unfortunately, this 'natural' account doesn't tell us precisely which cards are trumps. It doesn't explain why something such as racial or gender equality can be viewed as a human right in one era, and denied in another. Nor does it tell us how to handle inevitable disagreements over the content of human rights. If people believe that human rights have a transcendent source, there are likely to be as many interpretations of what counts as a human right as there are gods and religious traditions. This is precisely the dilemma we confront around sexual orientation and gender identity when we seek universal protection for practices that continue to be viewed as immoral within many traditions.

A second philosophical approach is better equipped to explain why conceptions of rights change through time, but it makes more modest claims for human rights. In this 'political conception', human rights are produced by political practices; human rights exist because people and states have agreed that they should exist, not because they are universally valid moral precepts. Whereas many forms of discrimination (e.g. on the basis of race or gender) are now understood as violations of human rights standards, this is not because they were always human rights awaiting discovery by enlightened people; instead, rights have been created by political processes that established a deep international consensus in favour of equality. Until very recently, there was no international consensus that even the most horrific crimes justified intervention in the internal affairs of independent states. Only since the International Criminal Court was established in 2002 has there been any permanent mechanism through which the international community can prosecute those guilty of genocide, crimes against humanity and war crimes.

The 'political conception' of human rights offers a persuasive explanation of how human rights are formulated in the international system, but it is also inherently conservative: a claim will only become a *human right* when a preponderance of international opinion (as expressed by states) accepts it. Up until that point, controversial human rights claims are like agenda items that have been marked for discussion, but not for action. While the impulse towards equality that has driven previous international changes is now promoting acceptance of sexual diversity, there is clearly no international consensus supporting gay rights. And it is only when a very strong consensus exists that the international community begins to move towards *enforcement* of human rights. If international protection for gay rights is remote, what role can international human rights practice play while rights are still being debated?

Historically, an important function of international human practice has been to provide governments with a debating forum and to legitimate those voices that are calling for reform. The Universal Declaration of Human Rights contained no enforcement mechanism, precisely because states would not have accepted a declaration that recognized controversial claims such as racial equality if such rights were capable of being enforced. Nevertheless, the Universal Declaration's guarantee of non-discrimination on the basis of race helped transform laws and practices through indirect influence on judicial decisions, and by lending moral authority to actors involved in domestic struggles for equality. By giving a voice to human rights advocates and requiring states to explain and justify their conduct publicly, the cause of human rights has been advanced incrementally. For example, invitations to African National Congress representatives to address the UN were early steps in the international battle against apartheid.

Treaty making around subsequent controversial issues – such as the rights of women, of indigenous people, of persons with disabilities – has repeated this pattern. In each case, standard-setting and negotiation of conventions have been entirely separated from enforcement. Most international human rights conventions contain reporting requirements and mechanisms for 'periodic review' during which states discuss each other's compliance. In some cases, 'optional protocols' create individual complaints mechanisms. While participation in optional protocols is voluntary and the decisions of international legal bodies are frequently ignored, human rights treaty bodies do influence the development of legal norms within national and regional human rights courts. Some regional courts, such as the European Court of Human Rights and the Inter-American Court of Human Rights, carry greater authority than the global institutions.

Of course, international human rights practices can be reformed. It was the realities of power, rather than principle, that produced an international human rights process based on deliberation rather than enforcement: influential nations were reluctant to accept international meddling in their internal affairs. There is no doubt that deliberative international human rights practice is unacceptably slow to provide protection, and countless lives continue to be blighted by sexuality-linked persecution. Since many of the states that persecute sexual minorities are comparatively weak, it is tempting to hope that international pressures might accelerate social reform. However, as we try to improve upon this imperfect system in ways that protect vulnerable people, it is important to remember that interference might prompt harsher victimization. Those of us in privileged positions have a responsibility to consider the consequences of our actions for those who are most vulnerable.

The traps of well-meaning egoism

Rahul Rao describes the plight of third world queers, trapped between homophobic nationalist governments and the frequently misguided interventions of the 'gay international', with a phrase that he borrows from Hannah Arendt's account of Jews in World War II choosing between 'malevolent enemies and condescending friends'.[4] Since the relationship between western and third world activists will often be one of inequality, it is easy for activists to participate accidentally in a 'discursive colonization', which presumes that western concerns will be universal and so ignores the wishes of intended allies.[5] Consider a statement released by a group of African human rights defenders (including the late David Kato) in 2007 in order to discourage public participation in 'any LGBTI campaigns or calls to action concerning Africa that are led by Peter Tatchell or Outrage!'. They wrote:

> Collaboration across continents is both important and valuable. We are willing to work with those who respect our advice and expertise regarding our continent. However, Outrage! has been acting in contempt and disregard of the wishes and lives of African Lesbian, Gay, Bisexual, Transgender, and Intersex (LGBTI) Human Rights Defenders. Outrage! exaggerates the violations our governments commit. When they quote African Human Rights Defenders in the very same press releases where they are exaggerating claims against our governments, we are held responsible for their reckless outbursts. As African activists, we are then left to face the wrath of our communities for statements we never made.[6]

Tatchell rebutted these allegations, stating that he always works with local activists and that these criticisms arose from rivalries among African activists. Whatever the merits of the critique of Tatchell, the complexity of the situation is undeniable. President Obama's initial intervention in Ugandan politics – which President Museveni has claimed prompted him to sign the anti-homosexuality bill into law – is a similar example. Such incidents illustrate that it can be difficult for western activists to understand the cultural and political context of their developing-world allies, and too easy to subscribe to rescue fantasies that buttress racialized ideas about the western self.

After investigating the Tatchell incident, Rahul Rao speculates that some western activists, having achieved unanticipated success at home, seek out human rights abuses abroad in order to justify their activist identities.[7] He suggests this dynamic plays out at a psychological level for some activists, and in a more instrumental way for NGOs such as Amnesty and Oxfam that mobilize donations by highlighting the suffering of distant others. Since any progressive political impulse could be reduced to some kind of psychological egoism, it might be a mistake to make too much of this criticism: there will be a mixture of altruism and ego at work in most political action (for academic commentators such as ourselves, an international focus has both psychological and instrumental dimensions). Activism combines both expressive and pragmatic impulses, so it is important to think carefully about the possible consequences of any action.

At a minimum, progressive international activism should be guided by those most at risk, rather than determined by the feelings and psychological needs of western activists. The international campaign against Brunei when Sultan Hassanal Bolkiah introduced sharia law (discussed earlier) is a case in point. This activism was not requested or supported by people in Brunei; there was no reason to believe that a response from the 'gay international' would be productive, and nothing to suggest that sexual minorities were the sultan's target. The Hollywood stars who demanded boycotts of hotels owned by the sultan were engaging in 'feel-good' politics rather than acting in concert with regional civil society groups in Brunei.

Western gay liberation mostly arose alongside movements for racial and gender equality at a time of social tumult. It is possible that other queer activists will be able to seize similar moments of social awakening, as occurred through the integration of Hong Kong's 2014 pride parade into that city's 'Umbrella Revolution'. However, differing historical, political and cultural contexts mean that acceptance of sexual diversity may take different shapes in different societies. Alicia Izharuddin observes that political constraints mean Malaysia's dominant forms of queer activism are cultural (art exhibitions, film screening, fora, zine-making and music) and 'take place only in small, often rather exclusive pockets of urban centres, particularly in Kuala Lumpur'.

Nevertheless, this activism 'is significantly influenced by feminist ideals' and 'project[s] a consciously localised expression of queer politics'.[8] Just as Izharuddin rejects a 'universalized narrative of gay modernity', so too do many people reject the idea that sexual practice should form the basis for identity. 'LGBTI' identities have clearly been embraced by at least a significant minority within most societies, and it is important to respect the agency of people who choose to adopt 'western' sexual identities. But it is impossible to predict accurately the different ways in which societies might accommodate sexual diversity, and it is possible to imagine cultural configurations that preserve much greater space for sexual fluidity than is allowed by the western emphasis on discrete identities.

Towards international collaboration

It is clichéd, but mostly accurate, to observe that change must usually be generated within a society, rather than imposed from outside. While international discourses on gay rights may promote polarization amongst governments, often for reasons of realpolitik, they also nurture local activists and encourage people to think through new possibilities for themselves at a local level.

The hard work of queer NGOs, and their allies such as Amnesty, Human Rights Watch and the Open Society Foundation, is changing international discourses, albeit slowly, and while most unsolicited international interventions are unlikely to be successful, there are examples of productive international collaborations around sexual rights. In remarkably tough conditions, small groups of activists are forging new possibilities, and those of us in safer and better-resourced environments have a responsibility to listen and offer support on terms that local activists request, rather than assume there are universal blueprints to be followed.

Working through HIV and reproductive health programmes has sometimes proved the least disruptive way that outsiders can support cultural change. As Indonesian scholar and activist Dede Oetomo comments: '[i]n Cambodia, you can actually have something like a Pride Parade. But it is called the HIV and Awareness Parade.'[9] The local organization Gays and Lesbians of Zimbabwe faces constant threats of violence and police raids, but partnership with international public health bodies has provided an important means for raising larger issues of sexuality. AIDS Free World, based in Canada, has used arguments about the implications for the spread of HIV in challenging anti-homosexual laws in the Caribbean.

In many societies, activists are at pains to explain that organized homophobia has been introduced by colonialism or imported from the west, and that sexual and gender diversity existed within indigenous traditions. Efforts to recover cultural traditions that celebrated or accepted transgenderism and same-sex intimacy can be undermined by highly visible western promotion of 'LGBT' identities. As a report on conditions in Ethiopia suggests: 'Gay-identified men concerned about social exclusion are aware that if it is done badly, organising around SOGIE [*sic*] rights could be counterproductive by disrupting the official status of homosexuality as a non-issue... especially if some sections of government are keeping expressions of homophobic hatred at bay in a fragile and hidden process as some evidence suggests.'[10]

In analysing the failures of economic reforms promoted by international financial institutions, development economists have emphasized the importance of 'sequencing' reforms, so that certain policies are adopted only once other institutions are in place. 'Sequencing' might also provide a useful metaphor for queer rights. Promoting radical ideas or even too much visibility in communities where sexuality is not conceived as a legitimate identity may provoke a backlash that sets back sexual freedom. One can repudiate homophobia without claiming a 'human right' to same-sex marriage, as claimed by many gay activists. (Other activists have argued that 'marriage equality' is a conservative project that betrays the radical potential of queer politics.)

Most international LGBT organizations are aware that promotion of marriage equality can provoke a backlash, but the emphasis on marriage as the ultimate goal of the movement is strongly emphasized in television shows such as *Glee* and *Modern Families*. This in turn creates an easily appropriated scapegoat for conservative politicians and preachers in places where homosexuality is an unfamiliar, western identity. Societies in which intergenerational familial obligations are the primary form of social security commonly allow some space for sexual freedom; however, the idea of 'gay marriage' may draw unwelcome attention to homosexuality as a threat to the implicit social (and economic) contract.

Activism, like development, is an adaptive process in which interventions are most likely to be successful if they are led by local activists and serve to amplify existing progressive political forces. Our favourite, if parochial, example is the success of Sydney Gay and Lesbian Mardi Gras, mentioned in chapter 2: this moved from being a small political commemoration of Stonewall, which had little resonance in Australia, to an end-of-summer street parade and party in early March, now the largest such event in the national calendar. But there are many examples from across the world of queer activism, often in environments far more hostile than those faced in Sydney. If there is a reason for optimism today, it stems largely from the constant development of new forms of bottom-up demands for dignity and autonomy, symbolized by the bravery of campaigners for equality who lead organizations such as the growing trans* groups across Latin America, the 'LGBT' groups in Kenya and Uganda and Zimbabwe which continue despite constant harassment and persecution, or the women activists in China who identify as lesbian and risk social and political ostracism.

There are more and more examples of progress coming from movements in the global south, which suggest a variety of paths opening up for liberation. Argentina led the way in accepting trans* identities, which, as we have noted, are increasingly being recognized in south Asia, despite continuing anti-homosexual laws. The first political party organized specifically to fight for queer rights was LADLAD in the Philippines, which battled for a few years to win legal recognition before it could field candidates. Legal challenges are being mounted to overthrow existing sodomy laws and anti-homosexual provisions in the immigration statutes of Trinidad and Tobago and of Belize (rulings are pending at the time of writing).[11] Groups such as the Coalition of African Lesbians, and some of the current queer movements in Brazil, are forging new alliances with other progressive groups, which recognize the interconnections between inequalities based on class, race and gender as well as sexuality.

Celebrity advocacy for gay rights may be one area where productive intercultural dialogue is possible, although even here the evidence is mixed. Academic research offers some evidence that opinions can be swayed by public figures (Magic Johnson's public revelation of his HIV status is a thoroughly researched example).[12] However, even in an era of global celebrities, cross-national emotional identification may be too weak for many celebrities to exert much influence. Ugandan activist Frank Mugisha once suggested that the American rapper Jay Z could do more than anyone else to shift cultural attitudes in Uganda, but there is little evidence that Jay Z's repeated advocacy of gay rights and same-sex marriage (since 2012) has transformed Ugandan public opinion.[13] The explicit embrace of queer sexuality by western pop stars such as Lady Gaga and Madonna may well have consolidated value change among the most devoted groups within their international fan base, and Taiwanese pop idols such as Jolin Tsai and A-Mei are now playing a similar role in promoting acceptance across the Mandarin-speaking world. Popular culture contributes to slow cultural change; but while celebrities' participation in specific campaigns can raise the prominence of a particular issue, their influence is limited. Nevertheless, the presence of high-profile government representatives or celebrities at queer parades and festivals in countries where there is considerable anti-gay prejudice can provide important protection and morale for local activists.

International and regional human rights processes have also often been productive, albeit painfully slow. The 'Universal Periodic Review' of each state's human rights records, conducted every four years by the United Nations Human Rights Council, creates an opportunity for other governments and civil society actors (both domestic and international) to discuss issues of concern, which frequently include sexuality. In 2011, in a report prepared for the UN Human Rights Committee, Navi Pillay found that several states (including Mauritius, Nauru, Palau, São Tomé and Principe, and the Seychelles) had decriminalized homosexuality directly in response to recommendations from this review process.[14] (Mauritius, however, still retains laws against sodomy, alongside some anti-discrimination protections on grounds of sexuality.) Malawi, which has equivocated over sexual rights, assured the UN Human Rights Committee in 2014 that police had been instructed not to prosecute people for same-sex conduct while a constitutional review was under way.[15] On the other hand, in response to calls for decriminalization in Sri Lanka in 2014, government delegates claimed the national Constitution 'protects persons from stigmatization and discrimination on the basis of sexual orientation and gender identities', and that there was no contradiction between this claim and its continued criminalization of 'unnatural' sex and 'acts of gross indecency'.[16]

When politicians condemn other states' human rights records outside these formal processes, they often generate headlines, but rarely achieve positive outcomes. While the work of international 'periodic review' processes and the decisions of human rights courts often have a low profile, both have achieved success in consolidating existing social changes, and nudging action forwards, if painfully slowly. The obvious advantage of this incremental approach is that it avoids the kind of moral schisms, backlash and polarization that can be prompted by highly public moralizing.

Conclusion

Among the committee that met to draft the Universal Declaration of Human Rights in 1947, not a single member made mention of sexuality. While sexuality was not yet a subject of public discussion and periods of official homophobia blighted countless lives, the subsequent decades also experienced considerable law reform; across all regions, many countries progressively wound back criminal sanctions against homosexual acts, and movements towards tougher penalties were rare. While this general trend towards sexual freedom continues to this day, in the early twenty-first century a second trend emerged: some governments began to increase sanctions on homosexual behaviour and to deploy homophobia for political purposes. While we would love to end on an optimistic note, we fear that global disparities around sexuality will worsen before they improve. The vast inequalities between nations mean that the political demands of comparatively afflu-ent gay communities are deeply unpopular – or perhaps incomprehensible – to many people in developing countries. Such conditions will continue to create opportunities for authoritarian leaders to exploit fear and prejudice as a means of bolstering their control.

During negotiation over the UN Charter, there were heated debates about racial equality, recognition of which would delegitimize colonial possession and discriminatory domestic laws.[17] Who then could have predicted subsequent developments towards racial equality as at least a universal rhetorical norm? Likewise, fifty years ago, as the early gay liberation movement called for radical social transformations, few would have guessed that marriage equality would one day became a central gay demand, that sexual freedom would come to be framed as a 'human rights' issue, or that sexuality would be debated by state leaders and would come to polarize international human rights debates. Today it is equally impossible to predict the political configurations that might arise in future decades, and it would be a mistake to assume that history will lead to universalization of western modes. The current growth of fundamentalist religiosity in many parts of the world makes it difficult to assume progress is easy or even inevitable.

One reason for our caution is that the growing international polarization around sexual rights makes it more difficult for hostile governments and publics to change their views, because this will be seen as capitulating to external pressure. Our sense that open rivalry between governments is promoting polarization, while international social and cultural processes are slowly promoting tolerance, is confirmed by the experience of authoritarian states such as China, Vietnam and Cuba, which, without much public debate over sexual rights, are now inching towards acceptance of homosexuality, even if they remain hostile to any political mobilization based on claims for human rights. If countries such as Russia are to change their attitudes, it will not necessarily be through embracing notions of 'LGBT' identity, but rather, as Laurie Essig suggests, because 'There is a rich and beautiful tradition of sexual otherness in Russia, one that is full of the imagined community of "our people" without the strict imposition of binary and stable identities as straight or gay.'[18]

As the cover photo of Conchita Wurst suggests, there may well develop new global forms of fluidity in which neither sexuality nor gender is perceived as immutable. Conversely, while we may ultimately see near-global acceptance of the rhetoric of equality, this may hide ongoing persecution and prejudice which cannot easily be addressed through legal means. But as new generations of activists emerge in often appallingly hostile environments, it is likely that new forms of sexual and gender diversity will emerge that will challenge the essentialism of dominant sexual identities while expanding sexual freedoms.

Introduction

[1] Strudwick, Patrick (2014) Crisis in South Africa: The shocking practice of 'corrective rape' – aimed at 'curing' lesbians. *Independent* 4 January.

[2] Lorway, Robert (2015) *Namibia's Rainbow Project*. Bloomington: Indiana University Press: 39.

Chapter 1

[1] Wilkinson, Cai (2014) Putting 'traditional values' into practice: The rise and contestation of anti-homopropaganda laws in Russia. *Journal of Human Rights* 13: 363–79.

[2] Kong, Travis (2010) *Chinese Male Homosexualities*. London: Routledge; Jeffreys, Elaine with Haiqing Yu (2015) *Sex in China*. Cambridge: Polity: 68–95.

[3] Herdt, Gilbert H., ed. (1993) *Ritualized Homosexuality in Melanesia*. Oakland: University of California Press.

[4] Richardson, Diane (2007) Patterned fluidities. *Sexualities* 41(3): 457–74.

[5] For a discussion of this within southeast Asia see e.g. Boellstorff, Tom (2007) *A Coincidence of Desires: Anthropology, Queer Studies, Indonesia*. Durham, NC: Duke University Press: 191–6.

159

6   Aggleton, Peter and Parker, Richard (2015) Male sex work: Current characteristics and recent transformations, in P. Aggleton and R. Parker (eds.): *Men Who Sell Sex*. London: Routledge: 1–14.

7   Garcia, Neil (2008) Villa, Montano, Perez, in P. Jackson, F. Martin, M. McLelland et al. (eds.): *AsiaPacifiQueer: Rethinking Genders and Sexualities*. Urbana and Chicago: University of Illinois Press: 163–80 at 174.

8   Cooper, T (2012) *Real Man Adventures*. San Francisco: McSweeney's Books.

9   See http://www.jackhalberstam.com/on-pronouns.

10 Beachy, Robert (2014) *Gay Berlin: Birthplace of a Modern Identity*. New York: Knopf.

11 Bereket, Tarik and Adam, Barry (2006) The emergence of gay identities in Turkey. *Sexualities* 9(2): 131–51.

12 Muldoon, James (1979) *Popes, Lawyers, and Infidels: The Church and the Non-Christian World, 1250–1550*. Philadelphia: University of Pennsylvania Press: 5–13.

13 Epprecht, Marc (2013) *Hungochani: The History of a Dissident Sexuality in Southern Africa*. Montreal: McGill-Queen's University Press: 153–4.

14 Symons, Jonathan and Altman, Dennis (2015) International norm polarization: Sexuality as a subject of human rights protection. *International Theory* 7(1): 61–95.

15 Boellstorff, *Coincidence of Desires*: 165.

16 Weinberg, George (1972) *Society and the Healthy Homosexual*. New York: St Martin's Press.

17 Boellstorff, Tom (2014) Lessons from the notion of 'moral terrorism', in Thomas Stodulka and Birgitt Röttger-Rössler (eds.): *Feelings at the Margins: Dealing with Violence, Stigma and Isolation in Indonesia*. Frankfurt: Campus.

18 Mosse, George Lachmann (1985) *Nationalism and Sexuality*. Madison: University of Wisconsin Press.

[19] Bejel, Emilio (2001) *Gay Cuban Nation*. Chicago: University of Chicago Press: xiv.

[20] Freud, Sigmund (1955) *Group Psychology and the Analysis of the Ego*, in James Strachey (ed.): *Standard Edition of the Complete Work of Sigmund Freud*. London: Hogarth Press, vol. 18: 122–3.

[21] Donham, Donald (1998) Freeing South Africa: The 'modernization' of male–male sexuality in Soweto. *Cultural Anthropology* 13(1): 3–21 at 15.

[22] Howe, Alyssa Cymene (2002) Undressing the universal queer subject. *City and Society* 14(2): 237–79 at 264.

[23] Altman, Dennis (2003) HIV and security. *International Relations* 17(4): 417–27.

[24] Haste, Polly and Gatete, Terry (2015): *Sexuality, Poverty and Politics in Rwanda*. IDS Evidence Report 131, April.

[25] Fletcher, Martin (2014) The next Crimea? *Prospect* 19 June: 57.

[26] Abrak, Isaac (2014) Nigerian Islamists plant flag. *Age* 27 August.

[27] Schulman, Sarah (2012) *Israel/Palestine and the Queer International*. Durham, NC: Duke University Press; Gross, Aeyal (2015) The politics of LGBT rights in Israel. *Columbia Human Rights Law Review* 46(2): 81–152.

[28] Lichfield, John (2014) Front National fear of 'gay lobby'. *Observer* 14 December.

Chapter 2

[1] E.g. Díez, Jordi (2011) Argentina: A queer tango between the lesbian and gay movement and the state, in M. Tremblay, D. Paternotte and C. Johnson (eds.): *The Lesbian and Gay Movement and the State*. Farnham: Ashgate: 13–26.

[2] Frank, David J., Boutcher, Steven and Camp, Bayliss (2009) The reform of sodomy laws from a world society perspective,

in S. Barclay, M. Bernstein and A. Marshall (eds.): *Queer Mobilizations*. New York: New York University Press: 123–41 at 130.

3 Thoreson, Ryan (2014) *Transnational LGBT Activism*. Minneapolis: University of Minnesota Press.

4 Altman, Dennis (1994) *Power and Community*. London: Taylor & Francis; Parker, Richard (2011) Grassroots activism, civil society mobilization and the politics of the global HIV/AIDS epidemic. *Brown Journal of World Affairs* 27(2): 21–37.

5 Thoreson, *Transnational LGBT Activism*.

6 Lorway, Robert (2014) *Namibia's Rainbow Project: Gay Rights in an African Nation*. Bloomington: Indiana University Press.

7 Quoted by Bong, Youngshik D. (2009) The gay rights movement in democratizing Korea. *Korean Studies* 32: 86–103 at 97.

8 Wotherspoon, Garry (1991) *City of the Plain*. Sydney: Hale & Iremonger, esp. ch. 3.

9 Colebatch, Tim (2014) The quiet campaigner. *Age* 27 September.

10 Mepschen, Paul, Duyvendak, Jan Willem and Tonkens, Evelien (2010) Sexual politics, Orientalism and multicultural citizenship in the Netherlands. *Sociology* 44(5): 962–80.

11 Rahman, Momin (2015) 'Sexual diffusions and conceptual confusions: Muslim homophobia and Muslim homosexualities in the context of modernity', in M. L. Picq and M. Thiel (eds.): *Sexualities in World Politics: How LGBTQ Claims Shape International Relations*. London: Routledge: 92–107, at 96.

12 See Llamas, Ricardo and Vila, Fefa (1999) Passion for life, in B. Adam, J. W. Duyvendak and A. Krouwel (eds.): *The Global Emergence of Gay and Lesbian Politics*. Philadelphia: Temple University Press: 214–18.

13 Binnie, Jon (2014) Neoliberalism, class, gender and lesbian, gay, bisexual, transgender and queer politics in Poland. *International Journal of Politics, Culture and Society* 27(2): 241–57.

14 Ayoub, Phillip (2014) Contested norms in new-adopter states: International determinants of LGBT rights legislation. *European Journal of International Relations* 13(3): 1–39 at 17.

15 Ferrarons, Albert (2010) *Rosa sobre Negro*. Barcelona: Egales Editorial.

16 Lancaster, Roger (1994) *Life is Hard*. Oakland: University of California Press.

17 But see Hamilton, Carrie (2012) *Sexual Revolutions in Cuba*. Chapel Hill: University of North Carolina Press.

18 Anderson, Tim (2009) HIV/AIDS in Cuba: A rights-based analysis. *Health and Human Rights* 11(1): 93–104.

19 Rohrlich, Justin (2014) Cuba wants you to think it's a gay Paradise. It's not. *Foreign Policy.com* 3 July.

20 Howe, Cymene (2013) *Intimate Activism: The Struggle for Sexual Rights in Postrevolutionary Nicaragua*. Durham, NC: Duke University Press: 5.

21 Narrain, Arvind (2007) Queer struggles around the law, in Nivedita Menon (ed.): *Sexualities: Issues in Contemporary Indian Feminism*. London and New York: Zed Books: 52–90 at 54.

22 Fish, Isaac Stone (2015) Gay cruising in Modi's India. *ForeignPolicy.com* 6 February.

23 Bochenek, Michael and Knight, Kyle (2012) Establishing a third gender category in Nepal. *Emory International Law Review* 26: 11–41.

24 Ammon, Richard (2012) Gay life in Bangladesh. *Globalgayz.com* 1 January.

25 Gevisser, Mark (2014) *Lost and Found in Johannesburg*. New York: Farrar, Straus and Giroux: 158.

26 Sember, Robert (2009) Sexuality research in South Africa, in V. Reddy, T. Sandfort and L. Risple (eds.): *From Social Silence to Social Science*. Cape Town: HSRC Press: 14–31 at 15.

27 CAL Advocacy Blog (2015) About CAL. https://caladvocacyblog .wordpress.com/about.

28 Florida, Richard (2014) The global map of homophobia. http:// www.citylab.com/politics/2014/02/global-map-homophobia/ 8309.

29 Chua, Lynette (2014) *Mobilizing Gay Singapore*. Philadelphia: Temple University Press.

Chapter 3

1 Beitz, Charles R. (2011) *The Idea of Human Rights*. Oxford: Oxford University Press: 13, citing *Filartiga v. Pena-Irala* 630 F.2d 876 (1980), 881.

2 Seifert, Dorthe (2003) Between silence and license: The representation of the National Socialist persecution of homosexuality in Anglo-American fiction and film. *History & Memory* 15(2): 94–129.

3 Johnson, Paul (2013) Homosexuality and the African Charter on Human and Peoples' Rights: What can be learned from the history of the European Convention on Human Rights? *Journal of Law and Society* 40(2): 249–79 at 251.

4 Burke, Roland (2010) *Decolonization and the Evolution of International Human Rights*. Philadelphia: University of Pennsylvania Press: 128–9.

5 Paternotte, David and Seckinelgin, Hakan (2014) Lesbian and gay rights are human rights: Multiple globalizations and LGBTI activism, in D. Paternotte and M. Tremblay (eds.): *The Ashgate Research Companion to Lesbian and Gay Activism*. Farnham: Ashgate: 209–24; Ayoub, Phillip M. (2014) With arms wide shut: Threat perception, norm reception, and mobilized resistance to LGBT rights. *Journal of Human Rights* 13(3): 337–62.

[6] Moyn, Samuel (2010) *The Last Utopia*. Cambridge, MA: Harvard University Press: 9.

[7] Johnson, Homosexuality and the African Charter: 251–2.

[8] Lau, Holning (2004) Sexual orientation: Testing the universality of International Human Rights Law. *University Chicago Law Review* 71(4): 1689–720.

[9] http://www.yogyakartaprinciples.org. See Long, Scott (2008) *Two Novembers: Movements, Rights, and the Yogyakarta Principles. World Report*. New York: Human Rights Watch.

[10] Oetomo, Dede (2012) New kids on the block: Human rights, sexual orientation, and gender identity in southeast Asia. *Asian-Pacific Law and Policy Journal* 14: 118–31 at 121.

[11] African Commission on Human and People's Rights, Res. 275: *Protection Against Violence and other Human Rights Violations Against Persons on the Basis of their Real or Imputed Sexual Orientation or Gender Identity*, 55th Session, 28 April–12 May 2014.

[12] Johnson (Homosexuality and the African Charter) notes the presence of an anti-colonial argument in the landmark EU case *Dudgeon v. the United Kingdom* (1981).

[13] Petchesky, Rosalind (2000) Sexual rights: Inventing a concept, mapping an international practice, in R. Parker, R. M. Barbosa and P. Aggleton (eds.): *Framing the Sexual Subject: The Politics of Gender, Sexuality and Power*. Berkeley: University of California Press: 81–103.

[14] Gross, Aeyal (2013) Post/colonial queer globalisation and international human rights: Images of LGBT rights. *Jindal Global Law Review* 4(2): 98–130 at 104.

[15] Sanders, Douglas (1996) Getting lesbian and gay issues on the international human rights agenda. *Human Rights Quarterly* 18(1): 67–106 at 102.

[16] Thoreson, Ryan (2014) *Transnational LGBT Activism: Working for Sexual Rights Worldwide*. Minneapolis: University of Minnesota Press: 33–5.

17. ORAM (2015) About us. http://www.oraminternational.org/en/about-us.

18. Overs, Cheryl (2015) *BOOSHTEE! Survival and Resilience in Ethiopia*. Evidence Report 129. Brighton: IDS.

19. Mann, Jonathan M., Gostin, Lawrence, Gruskin, Sofia, Brennan, Troyen, Lazzarini, Zita and Fineberg, Harvey V. (1994) Health and human rights. *Health and Human Rights* 1(1): 6–23 at 20.

20. Wu, Zunyou, Sullivan, Sheena G., Wang, Yu., Rotheram-Borus, Mary Jane and Detels, Roger (2007) Evolution of China's response to HIV/AIDS. *Lancet* 369(9562): 679–90.

Chapter 4

1. Mohamad, Mahathir and Ishihara, Shintaro (1995) *The Voice of Asia: Two Leaders Discuss the Coming Century*. Tokyo: Kodansha International: 80.

2. Quoted by Obendorf, Simon (2012) Queer politics in the global city-state, in A. Yue and J. Zubillaga-Pow (eds.): *Queer Singapore*. Hong Kong: Hong Kong University Press: 109.

3. Lambevski, Sasho A. (1999) Suck my nation: Masculinity, ethnicity and the politics of (homo)sex. *Sexualities* 2(4): 397–419. See also Brankovic, Avram (1998) *Bosnia Revelation*. London: Gay Men's Press; Davidovich, Boris (1996) *Serbian Diaries*. London: Gay Men's Press.

4. Stemple, Lara (2009) Male rape and human rights. *Hastings Law Journal* 60: 605–1535.

5. Gevisser, Mark (2000) Mandela's stepchildren: Homosexual identity in post-apartheid South Africa, in P. Drucker (ed.): *Different Rainbows*. London: Gay Men's Press: 111–36, at 117.

6. Azimi, Negar (2006) Prisoners of sex. *New York Times* 3 December.

7 Weiss, Meredith L. and Bosia, Michael J., eds. (2013) *Global Homophobia: States, Movements, and the Politics of Oppression*. Urbana: University of Illinois Press: 6.

8 Broqua, Christophe (2015) Les pro, les anti et l'international: Mobilisations autour de l'homosexualité en Afrique de l'Ouest, in E. K. Tall, M.-E. Pommerolle and M. Cahen (eds.): *Collective Mobilisations in Africa/Mobilisations collectives en Afrique*. Leiden: Brill: 183–204.

9 Kucera, Joshua (2014) US and Russia fight proxy war over gay rights in Kyrgyzstan. *Diplomat* 23 October.

10 Bop, Codou, trans. Pincus, Jane (2008) *Senegal: Homophobia and Islamic Political Manipulation*. Africa Regional Sexuality Resource Centre Occasional Paper 1/08.

11 Hilderbrand, Lucas (2013) A suitcase full of vaseline, or travels in the 1970s gay world. *Journal of the History of Sexuality* 22(3): 373–402 at 397.

12 Bob, Clifford (2012) *The Global Right Wing and the Clash of World Politics*. Cambridge: Cambridge University Press: esp. ch. 3.

13 Levintova, Hannah (2014) How evangelists helped create Russia's anti-gay movement. *Mother Jones* 21 February.

14 Connell, R. W. (1987) *Gender and Power*. Sydney: Allen & Unwin: 186.

Chapter 5

1 Cowell, Frederick (2013) LGBT rights in Commonwealth forums, in C. Lennox and M. Waites (eds.): *Human Rights, Sexual Orientation and Gender Identity in the Commonwealth*. London: Institute of Commonwealth Studies: 125–44.

2 Usmani, Basim (2009) Pakistan to register 'third sex' hijras. *Guardian* 18 July. http://www.guardian.co.uk/commentisfree/2009/jul/18/pakistan-transgender-hijra-third-sex.

[3] Putin, Vladimir (2013) Presidential Address to the Federal Assembly. http://eng.kremlin.ru/news/6402.

[4] Horvath, Robert (forthcoming) The reinvention of 'traditional values': Nataliya Narochnitskaya and Russia's assault on universal human rights. *Europe–Asia Studies*.

[5] Klotz, Audie (1999) *Norms in International Relations: The Struggle Against Apartheid*. New York: Cornell University Press: 41–4.

[6] Sanders, Douglas (1996) Getting lesbian and gay issues on the international human rights agenda. *Human Rights Quarterly* 18(1): 67–106.

[7] United Nations Commission on Human Rights (1999) *Civil and Political Rights, Including Questions of Disappearances and Summary Executions: Extrajudicial, Summary or Arbitrary Executions*. Report of the Special Rapporteur, Ms. Asma Jahangir, 6 January. E/CN.4/1999/39

[8] International Service for Human Rights (2010) GA Third Committee deletes 'sexual orientation' from resolution on extrajudicial executions. http://archive.today/4wUv.

[9] Long, Scott (2005) *Anatomy of a Backlash: Sexuality and the 'Cultural' War on Human Rights. World Report*. New York: Human Rights Watch: 15. http://hrw.org/wr2k5/anatomy/anatomy.pdf.

[10] Lau, Holning (2004) Sexual orientation: Testing the universality of international human rights law. *University Chicago Law Review* 71(4): 1689–720.

[11] International Service for Human Rights (2011) GA restores sexual orientation into EJEs resolution, adopts key texts on death penalty, Iran, DPRK. http://www.ishr.ch/general-assembly/983-ga-reintroduces-sexual-orientation-reference-into-ejes-resolution-adopts-key-texts-on-death-penalty.

[12] Resolution 17/19, UNHRC 2011.

[13] Ayoub, Phillip and Paternotte, David (2014) Introduction, in Phillip Ayoub and David Paternotte (eds.): *LGBT Activism and the*

Making of Europe: A Rainbow Europe? Basingstoke: Palgrave Macmillan, 1–25.

[14] Svensson, Jakob (2000) When is foreign aid policy credible? Aid dependence and conditionality. *Journal of Development Economics* 61(1): 61–84.

[15] Killick, Tony (1997) Principals, agents and the failings of conditionality. *Journal of International Development* 9(4): 483–95.

[16] UNICEF (2014) Eliminating discrimination against children and parents based on sexual orientation and/or gender identity. *Current Issues* 9.

[17] Bergenfield, Rachel and Miller, Alice (2014) *Queering International Development? An Examination of New 'LGBT Rights' Rhetoric, Policy, and Programming among International Development Agencies.* New Haven: Jackson Institute for Global Affairs.

[18] European Parliament (2010) Resolution RC-B7-0693/2010, 15 December 2010. http://www.europarl.europa.eu/sides/getDoc.do ?pubRef=-//EP//TEXT+TA+P7-TA-2010-0482+0+DOC+XML +V0//EN.

[19] African, Caribbean and Pacific Group of States (2010) Declaration of the 21st Session of the ACP Parliamentary Assembly on the Peaceful Co-Existence of Religions and the Importance given to the Phenomenon of Homosexuality in the ACP–EU Partnership. African, Caribbean and Pacific Group of States, 20 October. http:// www.lgbt-ep.eu/wp-content/uploads/2010/11/20100928-ACP -unilateral-declaration-on-inter-religious-peace-and-homosexuality. pdf.

[20] Kretz, Adam J. (2013) Aid conditionality as (partial) answer to antigay legislation: An analysis of British and American foreign aid policies designed to protect sexual minorities. *Vienna Journal on International Constitutional Law* 7(476): 488–9.

[21] https://globalequality.files.wordpress.com/2011/11/statement-of -african-social-justice-activists.pdf.

22 Pakistan Voice (2011) Controversy over US support for LGBT in Pakistan deepens. *asiancorrespondent.com* 15 July.

Chapter 6

1 Shahani, Parmesh (2008) *Gay Bombay: Globalization, Love and (Be) Longing in Contemporary India*. Delhi: SAGE India: 288.
2 See e.g. McNally, Stephen, Grierson, Jeffrey and Hidayana, Irwan Martua (2015) Belonging, community and identity, in L. Bennett and S. G. Davies (eds.): *Sex and Sexualities in Contemporary Indonesia*. London: Routledge: 203–19.
3 Kabwila, Jessie (2013) Seeing beyond colonial binaries: Unpacking Malawi's homosexuality discourse, in S. Ekine and H. Abbas (eds.): *Queer African Reader*. Nairobi: Pambazuka Press: 376–92 at 385.
4 Rao, Rahul (2010) *Third World Protest: Between Home and the World*. Oxford: Oxford University Press: 191–2.
5 Mohanty, Chandra Talpade (1988) Under western eyes: Feminist scholarship and colonial discourses. *Feminist Review* 30: 61–88.
6 Monthly Review (2007) African LGBTI human rights defenders warn public against participation in campaigns concerning LGBTI issues in Africa led by Peter Tatchell and Outrage! http://mrzine.monthlyreview.org/2007/increse310107.html.
7 Rao, *Third World Protest*: 186–7.
8 Izharuddin, Alicia (2014) *Double Marginalisation: Postcolonialism, Queer Studies and Decolonisation as Metaphor*. Working paper. https://www.academia.edu/8317667/Double_marginalisation _postcolonialism_queer_studies_and_decolonisation_as_meta phor.
9 Oetomo, Dede (2012) New kids on the block: Human rights, sexual orientation, and gender identity in southeast Asia. *Asian-Pacific Law and Policy Journal* 14: 118–31 at 125.

[10] Overs, Cheryl (2015) *BOOSHTEE! Survival and Resilience in Ethiopia*. Evidence Report 129. Brighton: IDS: 25

[11] Tomlinson, Maurice (2013) HIV and Caribbean law: Case for tolerance. *Oxford Human Rights Hub* 29 August.

[12] Pollock III, Phillip H. (1994) Issues, values, and critical moments: Did 'Magic' Johnson transform public opinion on AIDS? *American Journal of Political Science* 38(2): 426–46.

[13] Senzee, Thom (2015) How Jay Z can change antigay attitudes in Uganda. *Advocate* 19 March. http://www.advocate.com/world/2015/03/19/watch-how-jay-z-can-change-antigay-attitudes-uganda?team=social.

[14] Pillay, Navi (2011) *Report of the United Nations High Commissioner for Human Rights: Discriminatory Laws and Practices and Acts of Violence against Individuals Based on their Sexual Orientation and Gender Identity*. A/HRC/19/41, 17 November. http://globalequality.files.wordpress.com/2011/12/a-hrc-19-41_english.pdf.

[15] http://www.ishr.ch/news/malawi-use-political-will-review-anti-homosexuality-laws.

[16] http://iglhrc.org/content/sri-lanka-government-says-lgbt-rights-are-constitutionally-protected.

[17] Lauren, Paul Gordon (1983) First principles of racial equality: History and the politics and diplomacy of human rights provisions in the United Nations Charter. *Human Rights Quarterly* 5: 1–26.

[18] Essig, Laurie (2014) Bury their hearts: Some thoughts on the spectre of homosexuality haunting Russia. *QED: A Journal in GLBTQ Worldmaking* 1(3): 39–58 at 53.

Index

Index

Index